Y0-AEC-017

A Guide to Effective Study

Edwin A. Locke, a joint professor of psychology and of business and management at the University of Maryland, began the investigations leading to this book more than five years ago. His conclusions regarding the essentials of effective study were based on information gathered from a wide variety of sources, including his own studies of several hundred college students and a thorough review of the existing literature on study skills. A Harvard alumnus with a Ph.D. from Cornell, Dr. Locke has published numerous articles in the fields of psychology and business administration and is a consulting editor to the *Journal of Applied Psychology.* His wife, **Anne H. Locke,** brings seven years' experience as a professional educator to her collaboration on the exercises.

A Guide to Effective

Study

Edwin A. Locke

University of Maryland

With exercises constructed in collaboration with
Anne H. Locke

$S\!P$ Springer Publishing Company/New York

Designed by Patrick Vitacco

75 76 77 78 79 / 10 9 8 7 6 5 4 3 2 1

Library of Congress Cataloging in Publication Data

Locke, Edwin A
    Guide to effective study.

    1. Study, Method of.   I.   Title.
LB1049.L62   371.3′02812   74-79409
ISBN 0-8261-1580-2

Printed in the United States of America

To my wife, Anne,
who knows what it's like to teach a good student

Contents

Part I.   Study Methods

Part II.   Study Motivation

Preface for Students

The purpose of this book is to teach you how to study. It describes the mental operations required for understanding and remembering the material you will encounter in your college courses. The book also describes typical student motivation problems and provides some suggestions for coping with them.

Mastering the principles and techniques described here will enable you to learn more efficiently and more effectively. And learning is, after all, the purpose of going to college. One practical benefit of mastering course material is, of course, higher grades. Since grades can affect your career opportunities both directly (in terms of job offers) and indirectly (in terms of being able to get into a desirable graduate school), developing effective study skills can lead to numerous long-range benefits.

Furthermore, this book can provide you with insights into your own values and style of functioning as they pertain to school and college. Such insights may give you a perspective on yourself that will enable you to appreciate your academic strengths more clearly and to correct your academic problems more easily.

This book is divided into two parts. Part I deals with study skills, and Part II with study motivation. If you think your main problem lies in the area of study skills, start at the beginning of the book and read through it in order. If, on the other hand, your main problem is one of inadequate study motivation, you are advised to start with Part II and to read Part I later.

Most of the chapters in Part I are followed by practice exercises. The purpose of these exercises is twofold: (1) to enable you to practice the principles learned in the chapter; and (2) to provide you with feedback regarding your degree of understanding of these principles. You will observe that, in most cases, no space has been left on the answer pages for your answers. *Please use your own paper* for writing the answers. Following the exercises, you will note that information is provided which will enable you to evaluate your own answers. Representative right and wrong answers, most of which were given by students who have previously completed these exercises, are included for the purpose of illustration.

You are strongly advised to complete the practice exercises if you want to derive full benefit from this book.

It is suggested that you attempt to complete no more than two or three chapters per day, so that you do not become saturated by too much new material in too short a span of time.

Preface for Teachers

When I began my own research on the subject of study skills more than five years ago, I simultaneously began to accumulate previously published and still-in-print books on the subject. At last count I had collected fourteen—and there may be more. The question occurs, therefore, why add another book to this collection? My answer is that while existing study skills texts differ substantially in length, scope, and quality, they all fail, in my judgment, to deal, or to deal in sufficient detail, with two crucial topics: (1) the nature of the mental operations required for effective study; and (2) study motivation problems and how to cope with them.

It is not enough to tell students simply to "understand," or to "ask questions," or to "recall" the material that they have read. One must explain to them *specifically* how to perform these operations and, equally important, how to know when they are or are not performing them correctly. As virtually all researchers in this field have observed, most students have no idea how to study effectively when they enter college. Those who survive do learn how, although often painfully and inefficiently. Others drop out in bewilderment, never having acquired even the rudiments of effective study skills. One purpose of this book is to teach the student these skills.

Similarly with respect to motivation, it is not sufficient to tell students to "be mature," to "set goals," to "keep calm" during exams, or to "learn from your mistakes." One must explain to them how to accomplish these tasks. Remarkably few students can even identify in conceptual terms the emotions they feel regarding college (or any other aspect of their lives). Fewer still understand the causes of their feelings; and even fewer have a rational, consistent code of values to guide their choices and actions.

While this book is not a substitute for psychotherapy or for the study of ethics, it does identify some principles that students can use to arouse and maintain adequate study motivation, to reduce the debilitating effects of some disrupting emotions, and to remove blocks to mental effort.

In accordance with the two emphases described above, the book is divided into two major parts: study methods and study motivation. These are not entirely separate problems, however. The fundamental goals of study are: *understanding* the material studied and *remembering* it. Other goals, such as the arousal and maintenance of study motivation (or the removal of blocks to motivation), are the means to these ends.

The principles identified in this book were derived from six sources: (1) extensive interviewing of individual students with study problems; (2) noncredit "seminars" and discussion sections on the subjects of study skills and study motivation conducted with small groups of volunteers, including both "good" and "poor" students; (3) feedback, in the form of answers given by several hundred students to questions about two preliminary versions of some of the chapters; (4) my own study experience and that of acquaintances; (5) logical inference; and (6) other study skills texts (although these were not a major source of information).

The chapters are short and to the point. They focus on "how to . . ." rather than on presenting statistical information or research findings that may have no action implications for the individual student. Feedback from more than 500 college freshmen on earlier drafts assures me that the chapters can be understood and applied by any interested student. They are addressed primarily to college freshmen and to high school seniors planning to attend college, although others (both more and less advanced) may also find them helpful.

Most of the chapters in Part I are followed by practice exercises which the students are to complete using their own paper. Information is also provided to enable the students to evaluate their own answers. The teacher may want to collect these answers and evaluate them himself, or he may want to develop his own exercises for the students to work on.

I have specifically chosen not to cover such topics as writing papers (which would require a whole book in itself), how to study specific subjects (which is too specialized), or how to improve reading speed (which is too often obtained at the price of understanding). The emphasis of this book is on presenting principles that can be applied to any subject or type of reading.

Acknowledgments

I should like to express my gratitude to Dr. Arthur S. Mode for his assistance on all chapters of this book. I am also indebted to Dr. Allan Blumenthal, who made many pertinent comments on one chapter. Neither of these individuals is, of course, responsible for the contents of this book. I am especially indebted to Anne H. Locke for her assistance on all chapters of this book. Special thanks must go to the two students who spent considerable time and effort on the autobiographies in Chapter 20. Their names must go unmentioned in the interest of anonymity. Finally, I owe much to the hundreds of students who read (or listened to) and commented on earlier drafts of this manuscript. I learned a great deal from these comments.

Acknowledgments

Part I
Study Methods

1. Introduction

National statistics indicate that only about half of the students who enter college each year succeed in attaining a college degree. Whether those who fail to graduate are academically dismissed or leave of their own accord in anticipation of dismissal, their academic performance is typically poor. This poor performance, however, is rarely caused by lack of sufficient academic ability. Many college dropouts have quite high scholastic aptitude. In contrast, many of those who graduate have low aptitude scores. I know one student, for example, whose predicted grade average, based on his college aptitude test scores, was close to F. Despite this apparent lack of ability, he achieved close to an A average in college and went on to law school.

Furthermore, there is evidence that poor scholastic performance is not caused solely by an inadequate amount of time spent in study. It also depends on the quality of the time spent.[1] The facts indicate that unsuccessful students use inadequate, incorrect, and inefficient methods of study. As a result, they understand little of what they study and remember little of what they understand. Since the purpose of going to college is to learn (i.e., to grow in one's

1. F. P. Robinson, *Effective Study* (New York: Harper & Row, 1970), p. 81.   **3**

knowledge and in one's ability to think logically), this means that many students are simply wasting their time and money by going.

College Versus High School

The need for effective study skills is significantly greater in college than in high school. The failure to recognize this need leads many students into academic difficulty early in their first semester. Some estimates indicate that up to 40 percent of entering freshmen never make it past the first year.

There are at least four major differences between high school and college which dictate the need for more effective study skills in the latter.

Difficulty Not surprisingly, college is more difficult than high school. This is manifested in many different ways: there is a great deal more reading required; the material studied is more advanced and more complex; students may be responsible for a great deal of lecture material in addition to the required reading; the exams cover more material; exam questions are more demanding and answers are graded less leniently; there is more paper writing (at least for those in the liberal arts fields); papers are longer and the quality of writing and scholarship demanded is higher. Because the typical college student is older, more intelligent, and more knowledgeable than the typical high school student, college teachers logically expect more of him.

Since college is more difficult, it means that harder work and more effective methods of study are required to benefit from and to get through college than were needed in high school.

The average college student spends 20 hours a week in outside preparation[2] and attains a high C average. How does this compare with the amount of preparation and the grades you obtained in high school? And what does your answer imply about what you will need to do in college to attain the average you want?

Structure While high schools differ greatly among themselves, they are generally more structured than colleges. In college there are generally fewer total class hours (the average college student spends 19 or less hours in class and lab)[3]; there is less daily monitoring of

2. W. Pauk, *How to Study in College* (Boston: Houghton Mifflin, 1962), p. 5.
3. Ibid.

your progress in class; there are rarely any formal review sessions during class periods; class attendance itself is usually not required; quizzes are less frequent; what the student is expected to learn from the assignments may be specified in less detail (if at all); and paper topics may be less explicit. Owing to the larger student body and average class size, college is more impersonal; there is less contact with teachers and therefore less help and guidance from them.

Since college is less structured than high school, it means that a greater responsibility is placed on the student for independent, self-regulated study.

Long-Range Planning   Accompanying the reduced structuring of the college environment are increased demands on the student for long-range planning. Examinations are typically scheduled weeks or even months in advance with teachers making no special effort to warn the student when to start preparing for them. Term papers may be assigned which require weeks or months of research. Several exams and/or papers may occur or be due on the same day. Final exams may cover a whole semester's work. Thus long advance preparation is crucial in order to avoid being hopelessly swamped as the semester nears an end (if not sooner).

To meet college requirements successfully, the student must have a long-range time perspective. The capacity to attain and hold such a perspective is one of the hallmarks of psychological maturity. The student who believes that "the future is not real to me" (as one student put it) will not be able to cope successfully with the demands of college study.

Objectivity   It is becoming increasingly fashionable in high schools (as well as in the lower grades) for teachers to use subjective rather than objective criteria for determining students' grades. Grades are no longer being based solely on the student's demonstrated mastery of the course material; they are also determined by such criteria as whether the teacher personally likes the student or not; how much "effort" the student puts into the course; what effect the teacher thinks a certain grade will have on the student's "morale" (whether it will make him "feel" good or not); whether the student "needs" a high grade; "innate potential"; special "deals" like taking the exam twice; and promises of future achievements or memories of past achievements—all of these rather than actual performance in the course.

While subjective factors are not entirely absent in college grading, they tend to be far less prevalent than in high school. Even if a college teacher is prone to such biases, the larger, more impersonal classes, the frequent use of multiple-choice exams, and the use of teaching assistants as graders usually prevents him from acting on them. In college you will be graded basically the same way as everyone else—i.e., according to your demonstrated knowledge of the course material.

Summary

Most students who fail to graduate from college do so because they use ineffective study methods. Developing proper study methods is especially important for the entering college student because of four ways in which college differs from high school. College is more difficult, less structured, requires more long-range planning, and is more objective with respect to grading than high school.

2. What Is Studying?

Study is defined as the "application of the mental faculties to the acquisition of knowledge."[1] What does this definition mean? It states or implies that (1) studying involves the use of one's *mind*; (2) it requires the application of mental *effort*; and (3) it is a *means* by which one learns or gains knowledge.

(There are no effortless short-cuts to learning, including drugs. Most of the drugs popular among students today, including alcohol, impair rather than enhance cognitive functioning. They may cause perceptual illusions or hallucinations, reduced attentiveness, diminished capacity to estimate time, impaired memory, slowed reaction time, decreased capacity for logical, purposeful thought, or several of these at once.[2] Some of these drugs produce significant changes in mood or feeling. Neither the so-called "highs" which are actually due to the relief of anxiety, nor the "lows," which may also occur after the drug wears off, when the drug-taker realizes that his

1. *Webster's Seventh New Collegiate Dictionary.*
2. One drug group, the amphetamines, is an exception to the above, since when used properly it works as a stimulant and increases alertness. However, when used improperly, this drug can result in serious consequences, including addiction.

7

problems have not disappeared, are conducive to effective study.)

Part I of this book is addressed to the student who is willing to exert the mental effort that study requires. It will describe and explain the mental operations which he needs to perform in order to understand and retain the material presented in his courses.

Studying and Reading

Most of a student's knowledge in school is acquired from books and lecture notes, that is, through reading. *Reading is the process of visually (or tactually) perceiving and grasping the meaning of written language.* The process of visual perception itself requires no mental effort for an adult. To look at the words is to see them. Perception is governed by automatic physiological, biochemical processes in the brain and nervous system. The process of *grasping the meaning* of written language, however, as every student knows from his own experience, is *not* automatic. To see a word or sentence or phrase is not necessarily to understand it. To move one's eyes over a written page is not inevitably to know its meaning.

Levels of Reading

It will help to illustrate the difference between perceiving and understanding if we distinguish four different levels of reading.

Perceptual "Reading"   Read the following sentence:

> Der Weihnachtsabend in der von vier jungen Künstlern
> bewohnten armseligen Mansarde wird sich kaum von
> andern Abenden unterscheiden . . .

If you do not know German, you did not understand a word of the foregoing sentence. You were able to see the letters and words on the page, but you had no idea what they meant. You were perceiving but not understanding.

Unfortunately, many students read English as if it were an unknown language. If you get to the end of a paragraph or the end of a page and your mind is a total blank (or focused on a completely different subject), so that you do not have the slightest idea what you just read, the chances are you were doing perceptual-level "reading." (Another possibility is that the material was extremely difficult or poorly written, but to discover this you still must be in full focus.)

The word "reading" is put in quotation marks here because perceptual-level "reading" is not really reading at all. It is just looking.

(Now without reading back, what were the two previous paragraphs about? If you do not know, you were probably doing perceptual-level reading. Better go back and read them again!)

Now that you know what perceptual-level "reading" is, consider the following questions: Did you characteristically engage in perceptual-level "reading" in high school? What implications does your answer have for what you will need to do in college?

Reading requires something more than simple perception. It requires that you understand what the words *mean*—that is, what they refer to. The simplest type and lowest level of reading for meaning is called concrete-bound reading.

Concrete-bound Reading "George Washington was the first president of the United States." "Victor Hugo was a French novelist who wrote *The Man Who Laughs*." "Da Vinci painted the Mona Lisa." "Fifty percent of U. S. citizens earn over $8,000 a year." "Aristotle was a Greek philosopher."

All of these sentences refer to concrete facts. That is, they refer to descriptions of individual objects, persons, or events without direct reference to any new or complex abstract principles or definitions. The average student will generally understand such phrases simply by paying attention as he reads. He will know what the words mean, because they refer to simple concepts or to previously learned concepts.

Some reading in school and college is necessarily and appropriately done at this level, especially in introductory or survey courses (e.g., history, psychology, zoology) where basic factual material is emphasized. Such material forms the foundation for more advanced learning. Much material of this type need only be "memorized" for tests since understanding can be taken for granted.

Skimming or skim-reading is a form of rapid, selective concrete-bound reading where the purpose is to sample (but not necessarily understand) the content of a particular passage or chapter or book. The reasons for skimming vary. One may be looking up a particular fact, or trying to decide whether or not a book or chapter is worth reading at all, or be "previewing" a chapter one intends to read more carefully in order to know what to expect.

Speed-reading is a systematic form of skimming where the purpose is to get a very rapid overview of the basic factual content of some selection. Speed-reading may be adequate in cases where there is no need to retain the material for any length of time and where a thorough understanding of the material and integrations with other material are not required (e.g., pleasure reading, reading some magazines).

Was concrete-bound reading adequate for most of your high school courses? For a substantial proportion of your college studying, concrete-bound reading (including skimming and speed-reading) will not be adequate. Understanding most college material requires a higher level of reading.

Abstract Reading   Abstract reading is required when you encounter new and/or complex concepts, ideas, theories, or principles. It is aimed at gaining at least a minimal understanding of the meaning of such concepts or ideas. Such understanding will require a recognition of some relationship among groups of facts or less complex concepts on which the new concept is based or from which it is derived.

Assume, for example, that you had never before encountered the concept of "car" and were offered the following definition: "a car is a three- or four-wheeled, self-propelled vehicle designed to transport passengers across a solid, smooth surface. Some examples of cars are: Volkswagens, Chevrolets, Fords, and Cadillacs."

To understand this definition you would have to grasp the characteristics which were possessed in common by all of the specific examples of cars given (as well as those makes not given) e.g., three- or four-wheeled, self-propelled, etc. It would not be sufficient simply to remember a few specific makes. If you were asked, for instance, to define the concept of car and gave as your answer "a car is like a Volkswagen or a Ford," this would not show that you really understood the concept, since you did not name the attributes which *all* cars have in common. The latter definition would indicate that you had been doing concrete-bound reading (reading for isolated facts) rather than abstract reading (reading for understanding new concepts).

A related type of inappropriate concrete-bound (and partially perceptual-level) reading occurs when you memorize the words involved in some definition, theory, or principle without understanding the meaning of the facts or concepts to which they refer. For example, consider the chemical formula for water: H_2O. You could memorize this formula simply by doing concrete-bound reading (and rereading). But you could not claim to have attained any abstract understanding of the formula unless you could explain what it meant, i.e., that water is composed of two atoms of hydrogen and one atom of oxygen. (A full understanding of the formula would require that you also grasp what the terms "hydrogen," "oxygen," and "atom" mean.)

With the distinction between concrete-bound and abstract reading in mind, read the following passage for abstract understanding:

> The joint-stock company was an important instrument in the great English commercial expansion of the sixteenth and seventeenth centuries. The origins of the institution are to be found in the Middle Ages. The merchants and industrialists of fifteenth-century Italy developed the business technique of pooling capital resources to expand operations and distribute risk, and later English merchants no doubt borrowed somewhat from the Italian idea. . . .
>
> A typical joint-stock charter of this time gave the company a name and a formally recognized legal position, and specified the terms of organization. The charter vested control in a council . . . the membership of this body varied from six to more than twenty, and the direction of the affairs of the company was in its hands. . . . Membership in the company was secured through stock ownership. . . .
>
> Most famous of all was the East India Company, chartered in 1600. . . . This concern eventually became . . . the medium through which [the] English . . . penetrated India and wrested control of that great subcontinent from the Portugese, the Dutch, and the French . . .
>
> A. H. Kelley and W. A. Harbison, *The American Constitution* (New York: Norton, 1963), pp. 8–9.

Now, reading back as much as you wish, define the term "joint-stock company." Write down your definition on a separate sheet of paper before reading on.

Was your answer something like the following: "A joint-stock company is like the East India Company"? If so, you were doing concrete-bound rather than abstract reading, since you gave an example rather than a definition. A proper definition, based on the above passage, would be more or less like the following: "A joint-stock company was a method used by Englishmen in the sixteenth and seventeenth centuries to foster commercial expansion by pooling resources at the same time as distributing risk. The companies were composed of stockholders and had formal legal status. They were run by councils with 6 to 20 members."

If you have trouble reading for abstract understanding, details as to how to do it will be presented in the next chapter. But first, we must identify one additional and still more advanced type of reading.

Abstract Integrative Reading   Abstract reading requires some degree of integration in that the characteristics possessed in common by specific objects (e.g., certain four-wheeled vehicles) must be grasped in order to form and to understand the meaning of a concept (e.g., car). However, when concepts themselves are to be connected and interrelated, a higher level of integration—and therefore a more advanced form of reading—is called for. This may be called abstract integrative reading. It involves relating concepts or ideas to other concepts or ideas, e.g., other ideas reported in the same chapter, in other chapters in the same book, in other books, ideas presented in lectures, knowledge which the student has gained from personal experience, from his own reasoning, etc. Integrative reading presupposes that one has done abstract reading (or at least has grasped the individual concepts involved by some means), since one cannot integrate concepts which one does not understand. But integrative reading involves going beyond abstract reading just as abstract reading goes beyond concrete-bound reading. Integrative reading is the "highest" type of reading in that it involves organizing one's concepts into a meaningful picture.

Observe, for example, how a student who had grasped the meaning of the concept "car" could integrate this knowledge with other concepts. For one, he might consider in what ways cars are similar to and different from other types of moving vehicles (e.g., bicycles, motorcycles, planes, tanks, jeeps, trucks, etc.). He might also examine the development that led to the adoption of the automobile as a means of transportation (e.g., Henry Ford's use of the assembly line to cut production costs). In addition, he could look at the effects of the development of the automobile industry on the structure of national economy, the growth of unionism, the development of the oil industry, and the proliferation of vacation resorts. He could compare the automobile with other modes of transportation and might even make predictions about future technological developments in the automotive field. The list could be expanded almost indefinitely.

No student, of course, would or could make all of the integrations listed above in one sitting, since this would require weeks or months of research. The number and type of integrations that a student should make in a given course depends on several factors. One is the nature of the course material. If the material consists mainly of lists of unrelated facts, fewer integrations are possible than if the reading involves many complex abstractions. A second factor is the type of exams given. If the exams are mainly of the multiple-choice or true-false variety, concrete-bound plus some abstract reading should suffice. If the teacher gives short essay exams plus definition questions, abstract reading plus some integrative reading is advisable. If the exams involve problem-solving or long essays (or if the reading is being done for the purpose of writing a term paper), extensive abstract integrative reading is a must. Details as to how to go about abstract integrative reading will be given in Chapter 4.

Summary

Studying is a process of acquiring knowledge by the application of mental effort, a process which cannot be short-cut or bypassed (e.g., by the use of drugs). Most new knowledge which a student acquires comes from reading, or, more precisely, from the mental operations which he performs on the material he reads. Reading can be done at different levels. The student should never read at the perceptual level; this is not reading but looking. The student should read at the concrete-bound level only when he is looking for specific, isolated facts. The student should usually read at the levels of abstract understanding and abstract integration. The former involves grasping the meaning of (new) concepts, theories, or ideas. The latter involves connecting and relating the concepts encountered with each other and with prior knowledge.

EXERCISES

1. In your own words, describe briefly the difference between concrete-bound and abstract reading.

2. What kind of reading is required to answer question 1?

3. The following paragraphs describe how an imaginary student might read each of several reading selections. First the selection is given, then the description of how the student went about reading it is given. Label each description as either *concrete-bound, abstract,* or *abstract integrative,* according to which type of reading the imaginary student used. After each answer, *give the reasons for your decision.* If the student is reading at more than one level, indicate the *highest* level reached.

> **Corporations** As industries grew larger in the 1800's, another form of business organization, the *corporation,* became more common. It gradually became the leading form of business organization in the United States.
>
> To start a corporation, three or more persons must apply to a state legislature for a *charter,* or license, to start a specific business enterprise. Once granted, this charter allows the interested persons to organize a corporation and sell shares of *stock,* or certificates of ownership, to raise the capital needed to carry on the enterprise. The *stockholders* or *shareholders*—those who invest their money in the enterprise—may periodically receive *dividends,* that is, a share of the corporation's profits.
>
> L. Todd and M. Curti, *Rise of The American Nation* (New York: Harcourt Brace Jovanovich, 1972), p. 471.

a. As the student read, he thought: "A corporation needs three or more people plus a charter, and it sells stock for which dividends may be paid. . . . If you don't need a charter in order to start either an individually run business or a partnership, why is a charter necessary in order to form a corporation?"

> The untenanted ruins endure in Mesa Verde National Park. From May 15 to October 15 ranger-guides conduct tours of some of the outstanding ruins. During the remainder of the year, visitors can look down into the great villages and the small ones from vantage points along the roads on the mesa. A great many artifacts were discovered by

> members of the ranching Wetherill family in 1888 and before the area became a park in 1906. A representative collection is in the fine park museum.
>
> *National Parks of the West,* by the editors of Sunset Books and Sunset Magazine (Menlo Park, Calif.: Lane Magazine and Book Co., 1965), p. 194.

b. As the student read, he thought: "Tours go from May 15 to October 15; artifacts were discovered in 1888; the area became a park in 1906; the park is on a mesa."

> ... the expression *interest rate* is equated to several different concepts. ... [One is] a market rate of return on loans, called a rate of interest on bonds, or promissory notes.
>
> A. A. Alchian and W. R. Allen, *University Economics* (Belmont, Calif.: Wadsworth, 1967), p. 437.

c. As the student read, he thought, "One meaning of the term interest rate is the percentage of the loan that is given to a person as payment for making the loan."

> Without Andrea del Sarto [sixteenth century] Florence would be deprived of her festal painter: the great fresco of the *Birth of the Virgin* ... gives us something which Raphael and Bartolommeo do not—the fine joy in being alive which men felt at the moment when the Renaissance reached its zenith.
>
> H. Wölfflin, *Classic Art* (London: Phaidon Press, 1961), p. 155.

d. The reader thought, "The *Birth of the Virgin* by Andrea del Sarto is a fresco; it gives us joy."

e. The reader thought, "In general, the people who lived during the zenith of the Italian Renaissance were glad to be alive, as shown in del Sarto's art. Today, many art works show man differently—as tortured and mindless. I wonder if the general attitudes of today's culture are different from those of the Italian Renaissance?"

Evaluating Your Answers*

1. An example of an acceptable answer is:

> Concrete-bound reading is reading for isolated facts.
> Abstract reading is reading for the concept that integrates
> and connects the facts.

The following are examples of poor answers to this question:

> Concrete-bound is strictly reading the facts. Reading
> the printed material and stopping there. Abstract reading
> involves associating what you are reading with other
> stored knowledge.

This is not correct, because it gives as the main characteristic of
abstract reading that the ideas read are associated with one's other
knowledge. This is the essential characteristic of *abstract integrative*
reading. The essential characteristic of abstract reading is gaining an
understanding of a *concept* or *definition*.

> The difference between concrete-bound and abstract
> reading is that concrete-bound reading uses simple words
> that most people understand and gives examples to make
> it clear. While abstract reading is describing a thing in
> general and for me uses too many words to get its point
> across.

Here the student stresses the amount of effort required to do the two
kinds of reading and his personal opinion about the number of words
used. He does not identify the objective difference between the two
types of reading.

> Concrete-bound reading involves reading a specific
> statement concerning one particular thing in the sentence.
> Abstract reading is just a generalization about a topic. It
> describes nothing in particular.

This is an error because abstract reading *does* deal with something in
particular, namely, one (or more) concept(s). Furthermore, abstract
reading entails gaining an understanding of what qualities a particular class of objects have in common (e.g., cars).

---

* The majority of the answers given in Part I of this book are based on
actual student responses to these and related questions.

2. Abstract integrative reading is required, because the reader must (1) understand the meaning of the concepts "concrete-bound" and "abstract," and (2) relate these concepts to each other.

3. The correct answers are:

a. "Abstract integrative," because the reader is (1) seeking an understanding of the concept(s), and (2) relating the ideas to his other knowledge (i.e., his understanding of other types of business enterprises).

b. "Concrete-bound" is correct because the reader is remembering a string of facts without an attempt to understand their wider meaning and/or implications.

c. "Abstract" is correct because the reader is reformulating in his own words one meaning of the concept "interest rate."

d. The answer is "concrete-bound," because the reader only mentions two isolated facts. He merely notes that the painting is a fresco and that it shows joy. He does not consider the meaning of such terms as "fresco" or "Renaissance." Nor does he relate any of the ideas in the passage to his other knowledge.

e. "Abstract integrative" is the answer because the reader is (1) noting some information about the concept "Italian Renaissance," and (2) is comparing this knowledge with his own observations regarding contemporary art.

3. How To Do Abstract Reading

Abstract reading involves attaining some minimal understanding of new (or only partially understood) concepts, ideas, principles, or definitions. There are at least four techniques that can be used to accomplish this goal.

Techniques of Abstract Reading

Establish the Proper Mental Set   Just as a computer will not function unless it is given the proper orders, neither will a mind. In reading for abstract understanding the programming involves establishing a mental set or goal that says, in effect: "What is this?" "What does it mean?" "What does it refer to?"

How are these orders originated? Every chapter which a student reads is about some specific topic. Before you begin reading, make a preliminary survey of the section. That is, look at the title, then leaf through the chapter, examine the chapter index, look at the main headings, the figures, the tables, the chapter glossary, and the questions at the end of the chapter—whichever of these are present. *File these terms, topics, concepts, and ideas in your mind as things* **18** *to be learned or as questions to be answered.*

Some study-skills experts suggest that the student turn *every* heading into a specific question to be answered. Topic sentences which begin paragraphs can also be used for this purpose. For example, a heading entitled "Motivational Factors Causing Poor Work Performance" would be turned into the question: "What motivational factors cause poor work performance?" The purpose of this process is to set your mind specific goals to be achieved *before* you begin reading.

Formulating reading purposes in advance will also help you to *anticipate the author* as you read. Such anticipation helps to provide a sense of continuity in the material and may stimulate attentiveness. For example, if the author says he will discuss "three causes of the American Civil War," after he has discussed two of them you should anticipate a third.

This procedure is somewhat difficult to follow in English courses where novels are assigned, because there are no headings within the chapters and no glossaries or indexes. But the student can still set himself certain basic goals; for example: What is the theme of the book? What is the writer's view of man? What is the plot? What are the main events of the story? Who are the main characters? What is the author's style? Often the course instructor will suggest directly or by implication what the student should look for in such readings. If not, you can always ask for such information directly.

Reformulate the Ideas in Your Own Words New terms and ideas and concepts are typically explained to the reader by means of other, already familiar concepts. Sometimes such definitions or explanations will be very easy to understand so that no further study of them is required. On the other hand, some definitions are very complex—or they may be given by implication rather than directly. In such cases the student should formulate or reformulate the ideas or definitions in his own words. An example would be the concept of "joint-stock company" described in the previous chapter. No formal definition was given in the selection so that the concept's basic meaning had to be discovered by isolating its essential characteristics from the various passages.

Making your own formulations or reformulations has these benefits: it insures that the concept is described in terms of other concepts that you already know, and it discourages rote memorization of the word sounds in the original definition or the substitution of concrete examples for a definition (i.e., concrete-bound reading). It is virtually impossible to (correctly) translate a definition or idea into your own words unless you really understand what it means. One way to test your ability to reformulate a concept in your own words is to see if you can explain it clearly to another person who is unfamiliar with it.

One caution: when you reformulate an already given definition be sure that your definition means *exactly* what the original definition means. Do not distort the actual meaning simply because it is easy or convenient to do so.

Form General Mental Images   Sometimes it will help you to grasp the meaning of an idea if you picture that idea or some aspect of it in your mind in the form of a generalized image. For example, if the concept was "car," you could picture in your mind a vehicle with an engine, four wheels, and passengers traveling along a road. You should *not* picture a *specific* make of car to the exclusion of all others. This would be too concrete-bound. The image should be a general one, stressing the attributes common to *all* examples of the concept.

For another example, read this passage:

> The head starts growing at a very rapid rate almost immediately after conception. By the time a baby is born, the head has already achieved more than 60% of its adult size. . . . The trunk is next in growth rate, and by the end of the second year it has reached a point halfway to its final length. During the second year, the legs and arms begin to grow in earnest, reaching the 50 percent point at about the fourth year. This progressive growth—first the head, then the trunk, then the legs—has been designated by the term *cephalo-caudal* (head-to-foot).
>
> D. Krech, R. S. Crutchfield, and N. Livson, *Elements of Psychology: A Briefer Course* (New York: Knopf, 1969), p. 27.

To help yourself grasp the meaning of the concept of "cephalocaudal growth," you could form in your mind the image of a baby growing, with the head growing large first, then the trunk and then the arms and legs. You could picture the baby as if it were a "human balloon" being slowly blown up, starting with the head.

Be cautioned that mental images should not be used to *replace* reformulation of the concept of your own words but to *supplement* it. The images serve to clarify what the words mean—that is, what facts of reality they refer to.

Be warned also that some concepts are so abstract that it will not be possible to form meaningful images of them (e.g., the concept of "morality"). You will have to deal with such concepts using the other methods described in this chapter.

Break Down the Material into Smaller Units   Anything you read will be composed of certain linguistic, grammatical, and author-made units. For example, a book may be divided into parts, and the parts composed of chapters. Chapters themselves may be divided into sections by means of subheadings. The subheadings will consist of paragraphs, and each paragraph is composed of sentences. Sentences can be broken down into individual phrases each of which is composed of single words.

Here is a helpful rule: when the unit you are trying to understand does not make any sense, break it down into smaller units and try to make sense of them individually. For example, if a chapter as a whole seems meaningless, attack each section separately, and try to understand it. If a section is puzzling, analyze the individual paragraphs which make it up. If a paragraph is incomprehensible, try to grasp what the individual sentences mean. If a sentence is unclear, examine the individual phrases and words. If you cannot understand an individual word, look it up in the glossary of your text; if there is none, use a dictionary. (Word meanings, of course, are also given by the context in which the word appears).

A book or chapter or passage that looks totally incomprehensible at first glance may be understood by any serious student using this method. Even readings in one of the most difficult academic subjects, philosophy, can be understood in this manner. Consider the following passage from the writings of John Locke. See if you can understand it by analyzing it one sentence (or phrase) at a time.

If MAN in the state of nature be so free, as has been said, if he be absolute lord of his own person and possessions, equal to the greatest, and subject to nobody, why will he part with his freedom, why will he give up his empire and subject himself to the dominion and control of any other power? To which it is obvious to answer that though in the state of nature he has such a right, yet the enjoyment of it is very uncertain and constantly exposed to the invasion of others; for all being kings as much as he, every man his equal, and the greater part no strict observers of equity and justice, the enjoyment of the property he has in this state is very unsafe, very unsecure. This makes

> him willing to quit a condition which, however
> free, is full of fears and continual dangers; and it is
> not without reason that he seeks out and is willing
> to join in society with others who are already
> united, or have a mind to unite, for the mutual
> preservation of their lives, liberties, and estates,
> which I call by the general name "property."
>
> John Locke, *The Second Treatise of Government* (New
> York: Liberal Arts Press, 1952; originally published in
> 1690), from ch. 9, "Of the Ends of Political Society and
> Government," pp. 70–71.

This passage contains only three basic ideas. The first sentence
poses the question of why man, who is free to do anything he pleases
in a "state of nature," would give up any of this "freedom." (The only
individual word or phrase that you might have trouble with here is
"state of nature," which means "not belonging to any society."
However, this term would have been made clear earlier in the book.)
The second sentence implies what the answer will be by pointing
out that in a state of nature an individual cannot be certain of
enjoying his rights because other people might not respect them.
The third sentence completes the answer by declaring that men are
willing, therefore, to unite with others into societies as a means of
protecting their life, liberty, and property.

Breaking down complex passages into smaller elements is not only
helpful as a method of understanding, it gives the student confidence
in his ability to understand in general. Thus passages that would
produce a feeling of helplessness and apathy if attacked as a whole
can lead to heightened confidence and a sense of mastery when
broken down into parts.

When a chapter or passage is broken down into units which are
attacked individually, there is of course a need to integrate the units
again so that the writer's chain of reasoning will be understood.
Integration is the subject of the next chapter. But first a warning
about errors to watch for when doing abstract reading.

Common Errors in Abstract Reading

There are four common errors which students commit when trying to
do abstract reading.

Overconcreteness   Overconcreteness is the result of concrete-bound reading (discussed in Chapter 2). It consists of reformulating an idea simply by giving a specific example of it rather than by giving its abstract meaning or definition (e.g., "a car is like a Volkswagen"; "a joint-stock company is like the East India Company").

Vagueness   The second common error is, in one respect, the opposite of the first. Rather than being too specific, the reformulations are too vague. Terms are defined so broadly as to be almost meaningless, e.g., "a car is a thing that moves." This definition would not, for example, distinguish between a car and a turtle.

"Cheating" on Yourself   A third error to watch for is the tendency to "cheat" on yourself mentally when going over a new idea or concept. There is a temptation to pass quickly over any idea that is not immediately self-evident, at the same time telling oneself: "Well, I sort of know it," or "I have a rough idea of what it means," or "I feel like I have the general picture." Such thoughts really mean: "I don't really understand it, but I do not want to bother to go into it further. I'll study it 'for real' later." Later, the same students say to themselves: "Oh, yes, I know that. I remember studying it before." Then on exams they wonder why all that "studying" they thought they did failed to pay off.

One way to avoid this error is to make a habit of understanding each concept the *first time* you encounter it. Sometimes it helps to force yourself to explain the idea out loud or to *write it* in the margin of your book or in a notebook. (See Chapter 5 for further details.) Remember, if you cannot explain the concept *in your own words*, you do not fully understand it.

Subjectivism   A fourth error is subjectivism, which, in this context, consists essentially of substituting one's personal wishes, feelings, or opinions for what the author actually said or meant. One student who had great difficulty in reformulating ideas in his own words stated his problem in this way: "Most often I want the meaning [of a concept] to be what I want it to be [rather than what it actually is or what the text says it is]." To illustrate this error with a specific example, consider the following passage from an economics textbook:

> . . . the expression *interest rate* is equated to several different concepts. . . . [One is] a market rate of return on loans, called a rate of interest on bonds, or promissory notes.
>
> A. A. Alchian and W. R. Allen, *University Economics* (Belmont, Calif.: Wadsworth, 1967), p. 437.

Suppose that a radical Marxist student were asked on an exam to define the meaning of "interest rate" and he gave as his answer: "Interest is a means by which the ruling class exploits the workers by forcing them to pay for the use of their own money." This would be a subjective answer, because rather than showing that he understood what was said about interest in the textbook, he offered his own (biased) view of the concept. While this example is extreme, it illustrates the essence of an error which is very common among students.

Understanding requires an unbreached commitment to objectivity—which, in the context of studying, requires understanding what the writer actually says or means. This is true *even if what the textbook says is blatantly wrong.* You are perfectly free to disagree with a definition or conclusion, but before you can *rationally* disagree, you have to understand what was said. Furthermore, college teachers are usually not interested (or not primarily interested) in your personal ideas but in whether or not you understand what you read. Thus expressing your personal views on an exam is inappropriate unless they are specifically requested.

The Problem of Time

If you have grasped the implications of this chapter, you are probably now saying to yourself: "This is all very well, but if I actually approached all my reading this way, I would never have time to get it all done." You are correct in inferring that abstract reading is considerably more time-consuming than concrete-bound reading. However, you should be aware of three considerations. First, you do not have to perform *all* the mental operations just described on *all* the material you read. How much you do will depend upon the difficulty of the material, the nature of the course, your own prior knowledge, and the depth of understanding that you need to attain. Second, unless you are taking very easy courses, you will *have* to do a substantial amount of abstract reading in order to do well in college. Third, the more abstract reading (reading for understanding) you do, the easier and faster it will become.

Summary

Abstract reading involves reading for understanding. It is required when the ideas and concepts you encounter are new and/or complex. Four types of mental operations will help the student to attain understanding: establishing the proper mental set after a preliminary survey of the passage to be read; reformulating the main ideas or concepts in your own words; forming generalized mental images; and breaking the material down into manageable units. Four common types of errors should be avoided: overconcreteness; vagueness; "cheating" on yourself; and subjectivism. Abstract reading is more time-consuming than concrete-bound reading, but it is necessary if genuine understanding is to be achieved.

EXERCISES

1. a. Survey the following selection briefly in order to set yourself reading purposes. Do *not* read through the passage in order to do this. A quick survey is sufficient before jotting down the purposes. Then read the selection with your reading purposes in mind. Use abstract reading when you read the selection.

> **Argumentum ad Ignorantiam**   This means the "appeal to ignorance." It has the structure: "P is true." Why? "Because you can't disprove it." This type of evasion often occurs in discussions which involve religious faith. Thus a man may argue that the Book of Genesis gives a literal account of the creation of the world. A skeptic may state that this account appears improbable to him, though he may also admit that he cannot disprove it. The religious protagonist then asserts, "You must now admit that it is true, for you cannot disprove it." This is the appeal to ignorance or inability to disprove. But inability to disprove is not equivalent to proof. Only evidence gives us proof. If we accepted this kind of substitute for evidence we should be required to believe that the Angel Gabriel visited the prophet Mohammed to inform him that God had decided that the Moslem religion was to supersede the Jewish and Christian religions. For how would you go about disproving this claim? We are not required to accept the improbable merely because we do not know how to disprove it. As cautious thinkers, we will

> withhold belief until we have positive evidence
> in favor of a proposition.
> **Begging the Question** This evasion, known in
> traditional logic as "Petitio Principii," consists in
> our pretending to prove something when actually
> we *assume* in the "proof" that which we are
> supposed to prove. "Why do I believe that Zilch is
> guilty? Because he is guilty." The evasion has the
> following logical structure: "P is true." Why?
> "Because P is true." The "evidence" here merely
> restates the conclusion. There is thus no indepen-
> dent relevant evidence whatsoever; we have
> merely assumed the truth of that which we are
> supposed to prove. The conclusion is used to
> establish itself.
>
> L. Ruby, *Logic: An Introduction* (New York: Lippin-
> cott, 1960), p. 141.

b. If you were able to answer the questions which formed your
reading purpose(s) what did you find?

c. Now go back through the selection and analyze it in more detail
by breaking it down into units (e.g., sentences or groups of sentences). Reformulate the main idea of each unit in your own words.

2. a. Briefly survey the following selection in order to set yourself
reading purpose(s). Again, do *not* read through the passage in order
to do this. Then read the selection, using abstract reading.

> *Of Aerial Perspective* . . . There is another kind
> of perspective which I call Aerial Perspective,
> because by the atmosphere we are able to distin-
> guish the variations in distance of different build-
> ings, which appear placed on a single line; as, for
> instance when we see several buildings beyond a
> wall, all of which, as they appear above the top of
> the wall, look of the same size, [and all seem
> equidistant from the viewer] while you wish to
> represent them in a picture as more remote one
> than another and to give the effect of a somewhat
> dense atmosphere. You know that in an atmos-
> phere of equal density the remotest objects seen

through it, as mountains, in consequence of the great quantity of atmosphere between your eye and them—appear blue and almost of the same hue as the atmosphere itself when the sun is in the East. Hence you must make the nearest building above the wall of its real colour, but make the more distant ones less defined and bluer. Those you wish to look farther away you must make proportionately bluer; thus, if one is to be five times as distant, make it five times bluer. And by this rule the buildings which above a [given] line appear of the same size [and equidistant from the viewer] will plainly be distinguished as to which are the more remote and . . . [thus actually] larger than the others.

From a manuscript on painting believed to be Leonardo da Vinci's, in E. G. Holt, ed., *A Documentary History of Art* (New York: Doubleday, 1957), vol. 1, p. 282.

b. If you were able to answer the questions which formed your reading purpose(s), what did you find?

c. Now go back through the selection and analyze it in more detail by breaking it down into units (e.g., sentences or groups of sentences). Reformulate the main idea of each unit in your own words.

d. Form an image or picture in your mind of the main idea of the above selection. Sketch or describe in words the image you formed. Remember that the image should include all relevant aspects of the idea.

3. Read the following selection.

Retinal* disparity occurs because the two eyes have different locations in the head. Thus, each eye obtains a somewhat different picture of the same object or situation. The right eye sees more of the right side of an object than the left eye; on the other hand, the left eye sees a bit more of the left side. This difference in the views obtained by the two eyes is referred to as *retinal disparity*. Retinal disparity provides important cues for depth perception. The difference in images obtained because of disparate eye locations can be

> demonstrated readily by holding a pencil six inches from your face and alternately closing one eye and then the other.
>
> N. L. Munn, L. D. Fernald, Jr., and P. S. Fernald, *Introduction to Psychology* (Boston: Houghton Mifflin, 1969), p. 177.
> *Editor's note: The retina is the inner lining of the eyeball.

Form an image or picture in your mind of the main idea of this selection. Sketch or describe the image(s) you formed. Remember that the image(s) should include all relevant aspects of the idea.

Evaluating Your Answers

1. a. Examples of acceptable reading purposes are:

> What is the Argumentum ad Ignorantiam? What is Begging the Question?

Here are examples of inappropriate reading purposes:

> What is the writer trying to get at? Have I heard of this before? What is the main idea? Who is this story or passage directed to?

This answer is inappropriate because it is not sufficiently specific. The paragraphs in the selection have headings, which give the reader something specific to go on, and which should be used to formulate purposes.

> It seems that the purpose of these two paragraphs is to present different ways of proof.

This is not a reading purpose. It is the reader's hypothesis, formed, presumably, *after* a preliminary *reading* of the passage; thus the point of setting reading purposes is missed.

> First I'll ask myself questions about the paragraphs themselves. Second, redefine the subject matter into my own words. Third, form mental images. Fourth, if I have difficulty with any of the material I'll break it down so I'll be able to understand it.

These purposes, which refer to how to go about abstract reading, need not be put in writing. One should write down purposes specifically related to the *content* of the passage to be read. (It is for practice in setting the latter type of purposes that this exercise was designed).

b. An appropriate answer based on the acceptable purposes given in 1a would be:

> The Argumentum ad Ignorantiam involves the attempt to prove something by appealing to the ignorance of one's adversary (by his inability to disprove it). Question-begging involves attempting to "prove" something by arbitrarily assuming in advance the truth of that which one is trying to prove.

c. Here is a summary of the main ideas contained in the selection:

> The Argumentum ad Ignorantium is using another person's inability to disprove an idea (i.e., his ignorance), as *proof* for the validity of that idea.
> —P is true because you can't disprove it.
> —Often used as "proof" for ideas in religion (e.g. truth of the Book of Genesis).
> —Logically wrong, because only *evidence* (not ignorance) can be offered as proof of an idea.
> —Consequences of making this error: we would have to believe all improbable ideas.
> Begging the Question is "proving" something merely by asserting it as a conclusion.
> —P is a fact because P is a fact.
> —Offers no evidence for the validity of the idea in question.

Here is an example of an incorrect reformulation of these passages:

> The paragraphs are similar in meaning. They both talk about methods of answers people will use to get out of trying to explain or understand something they have nothing factual on.

This reformulation is incorrect because it attempts to integrate the ideas in the two paragraphs without specifying the meanings of the concepts under consideration (i.e., the Argumentum ad Ignorantiam and Begging the Question).

> Argumentum ad Ignorantiam means the "appeal to ignorance." Its purpose centers around numerous discussions or debates dealing with religion and various

faiths today. However, the end result, since there is no specific evidence on these subjects, is that we must maintain faith even when proof is not evident.

This is an incorrect reformulation. The student has incorrectly concluded that faith is a substitute for evidence, although the passage clearly states the opposite.

2. a. An example of an acceptable reading purpose would be:

What is Aerial Perspective?

The types of errors shown under 1a would pertain to this exercise too (not using the headings, reading before forming the reading purposes, and using purposes relevant to personal motivation which do not deal with the material at hand).

b. An acceptable answer stemming from the above reading purpose would be:

Aerial perspective is a technique used by the artist to show the distances (from the viewer) of different objects which look as if they are on a single line. To make an object seem farther away than another object make it seem bluer and less defined.

c. Here is a summary of the main ideas contained in the selection:

—Aerial perspective is a technique in which atmospheric effects show relative distances (from the viewer) of objects which appear to be along a single horizontal line.
—A painter should make foreground objects their natural color and distant objects *bluer* (in proportion to their distance from the foreground) and *less defined* than near objects.
—One can also make inferences about the relative sizes of the objects in a painting where aerial perspective is used.

Here are some examples of poor reformulations of the selection:

The main ideas in this paragraph are to explain what aerial perspective is and how you show it with a brush. The author does a good job using simple terms to explain what it is and how it is done to show perspective on a great painting.

The above is not a good reformulation because it is too vague and contains irrelevant material. The reader has omitted the characteristics which *define* aerial perspective and added his personal evaluation of the writing style.

> In painting, when trying to make something seem as though it were at a distance, tint it, so to speak, with blue. The farther away it gets from the front object, the more blue should be added.

This reformulation is incomplete. It omits the name of the concept in question, as well as its full meaning. It leaves out important details such as making distant objects appear less distinct as well as bluer.

d. Here is an example of an image which would successfully illustrate the concept of aerial perspective.

This would be a useful image because: (1) the objects shown all appear to be on a single line across the picture, as specified in the selection; (2) it uses shading (to stand for blue) which gets more intense for objects farther in the background; and (3) it uses decreasing distinctness to show objects farther in the background.

This would be a verbal description of an appropriate image:

> I am on the peak of a mountain and I can see the tops of some other mountains [laid out in a row]. The farther away they are the more bluish their tops seem and the less sharp their edges seem against their background (the sky).

The image below would be inappropriate:

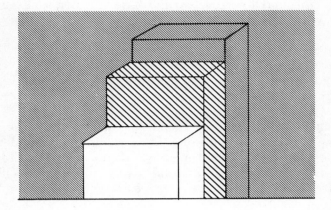

This image is inappropriate because: (1) the objects shown do not appear to be on a single line across the picture, but rather are placed along a line going into the distance, thus involving a different type of depth perspective; (2) the objects do not become less distinct as they lie farther away from the viewer.

3. The figure below is an example of an appropriate image:

It shows the same object from two slightly different angles, in accordance with what each eye would actually see.

4. How To Do
Abstract Integrative Reading

Integrative reading presupposes abstract reading (or understanding), because it assumes some prior grasp of the individual ideas and concepts being interrelated. Abstract integrative reading goes beyond abstract reading, however, in that it involves relating the ideas and concepts which you have understood to other concepts or ideas in the same chapter or text, to those in other texts, to lecture material, and to your own prior knowledge. It also involves deriving logical conclusions from the facts and ideas studied.

Since integrative reading presupposes and builds upon the knowledge derived from abstract reading, it leads to a deeper and more complete understanding of the ideas you encounter than does abstract reading alone. For this reason abstract integrative reading is the highest form of reading.

Types of Integrations

There are many types of integrations you can make with the material that you read. Some of the major types are described here.

Similarities and Differences A fundamental operation in the integra- 33 tion of knowledge is the identification of similarities and differences among theories, ideas, and concepts.[1] To illustrate, study the following passage, which describes two psychological "defense mechanisms."

THE DEFENSES AGAINST GUILT AND ANXIETY

Each individual strives continuously to protect himself from his feelings of anxiety and guilt. To do this, he makes use of a variety of techniques called *defense mechanisms*. . . .

Repression   The psychological process of repression is one of the most important of all ego defense mechanisms. By means of repression, the inner conflict at the unconscious level is not permitted to reach the level of consciousness . . . the unconscious life of each individual is made up of troublesome urges, strivings, and impulses which are constantly seeking to be expressed. Consequently it was necessary to assume the presence of some kind of critical, selective process which allows some urges to be expressed while others are held in check. At any given moment an individual does not express all the urges he carries about with him. He expresses only a selected few. The rest are controlled by the powerful forces of repression. . . .

Rationalization   Rationalization is a security measure by means of which a person avoids anxiety by justifying his deficiencies to himself and to others. It is a form of self-deception and mental camouflage. People make excuses and formulate fictitious arguments to convince themselves that their behavior is not so absurd and illogical as it actually is.

Aesop's fable "The Fox and the Grapes" is a

1. As implied in Chapter 2, integrating on the basis of similarities and differences is required for forming and understanding any concept and therefore is involved even in abstract reading. The types of integrations discussed in this chapter, however, are more complex in that they consist solely of interrelating concepts with each other.

> good example of rationalization. In this fable, a fox, who was fond of grapes, one day saw some luscious grapes on a vine out of his reach. He jumped for the grapes a number of times, but he was unable to reach them. He gave up in despair, and as he walked down the road away from the vineyard he said, "They were probably sour grapes anyway. Who wants sour grapes? Certainly not I!"
>
> G. W. Kisker, *The Disorganized Personality* (New York: McGraw-Hill, 1964), pp. 145–47.

Now answer the following questions on a separate sheet of paper. (You may look back if you wish, but do not look below at the answers until you have given your own answers.)

    a. In what important respect(s) are the concepts of repression and rationalization similar?

    b. In what way(s) are they different?

Here are some possible answers:

    a. *Similarities*: Both are types of defense mechanisms. Both aim at protecting the individual against guilt and anxiety.

    Both involve not being fully aware of one's feelings or motives.

    b. *Differences*: Repression is one of the most important mechanisms. (By implication rationalization is not).

    Repression is more strictly unconscious whereas there is a conscious aspect to rationalization.

    Repression is anticipatory in that it functions by preventing certain thoughts or feelings from entering conscious awareness; rationalization is more after-the-fact since it is used to justify some action that has already occurred.

The identification of similarities and differences can most easily be started by making comparisons among concepts within the same page or chapter of your text. Note that in the above example both items were discussed under a single subheading. Sometimes the writer will specifically state (or strongly imply) that two phenomena or concepts are similar or opposite in meaning and will leave it up to you to fill in the details.

But such comparisons do not have to stop within a given page. You can also compare and contrast material *in different chapters* of the same book and *between books in the same course*. It is also important to compare what is said in the *text* with *lecture* material in the same course. You can also compare and contrast the treatment of various topics in different courses and can also compare things you were taught in courses with beliefs or knowledge you possessed prior to attending college.

The analysis of similarities and differences can be applied to every area of study. For example, in studying French one could compare the form of the past and future tenses of two similar verbs; in mathematics one might analyze the similarities and differences between a sine and cosine; in history one could compare two theories of the causes of the American Revolution; in philosophy one could contrast two different philosophers' views on ethics; in English one might contrast the themes or styles of two novels or analyze the traits of two characters in the same novel; in psychology one could compare two types of mental illness.

When analyzing similarities and differences between ideas or concepts it is crucial to do so in terms of essentials (fundamentals), rather than in terms of trivial or nonessential factors.[2] For example, apes do not play checkers or produce movies whereas men do; but these are clearly not the essential differences between the two species. What is essential is man's possession of a rational faculty; this is the attribute that makes it possible for him to play checkers and to produce movies (not to mention the countless other activities engaged in by men but not by apes).

Categorizing and Recategorizing   The purpose of categorizing what you read is to organize the material in your mind. It may help to think of categorization as a type of *mental filing system* that puts the material into a logical order. You know that if office employees are to find and make use of the material in the files, the files must be logically organized. So must your mental filing system be logical and orderly if you want to be able to recall and utilize your knowledge effectively.

Virtually all written material that the student encounters is organized in some manner. The material in textbooks is typically

2.   For a discussion of some rules of definition, see L. Ruby, *Logic: An Introduction* (New York: Lippincott, 1960). For a related but different view see A. Rand, *Introduction to Objectivist Epistemology* (New York: The Objectivist, 1967).

categorized by the writer under specific headings and subheadings. If the material is already categorized, it may not be necessary to make any further categorizations. (However, you should be sure that you understand these categories and their interrelationship.) If the material is not categorized, you will have to do it yourself, especially if there are several different books in the course or if lecture and reading material need to be integrated. Sometimes you may want to recategorize the material in a new way that you think is more logical than that given in the book. (If you do this, however, be aware that on an exam your teacher may want only the categories given in the text).

How should you go about classifying the material in the book? The basic principle was given in the previous section, namely, *according to the observed similarities and differences among the concepts, ideas, or facts.* For any given idea or concept or fact you can ask:

—What wider (or broader) category does it belong in? What wider concept(s) can it be related to?

—What similar or related ideas, concepts, or facts belong in this same category?

—Can the concepts, ideas, or facts in the wider category be broken down into smaller or narrower categories? Can they be grouped into subcategories?

To demonstrate these points, examine the list of words below and then, on a separate sheet of paper, arrange them into appropriate categories and subcategories.

steak	carrots	pork
pears	food	peaches
vegetables	oranges	meats
veal	beans	chicken
peas	fruits	apples

You should have arranged the list as follows:

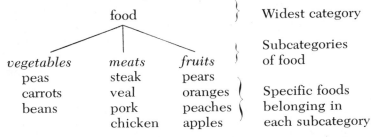

Note how the categorizing system helps to organize and condense the material in your mind. Instead of having to learn one long list of

15 separate, randomly ordered words, you would need only to learn three short, logically organized lists. Since the subcategories and the terms within each subcategory are interrelated, recall would be relatively easy.

Of course, the concepts you encounter in most of your reading will not be as easy to categorize as those in the above list (which are quite simple), especially if you have to think up the objectively appropriate categories yourself. On the other hand, as noted, the major categories may be given to you by the writer, so that your job would be simply to make sure you identify, understand and remember them.

These general rules will help you to categorize most efficiently:
—Do not put fundamentally dissimilar (or only superficially similar) things into the same category.
—Do not make too many categories (e.g., so that you end up with almost as many categories as you have things to categorize).
—Do not make too few categories (e.g., so that everything ends up in one or two categories when more are clearly needed).

Cause and Effect Relationships   Having grasped the specific meaning of an idea or phenomenon, one can ask certain questions about it. Two of these questions have already been discussed: how is it similar to other (known) phenomena; and how is it different from them? Two additional questions one can (sometimes) ask are: What are its causes? (Or: What is the evidence that led to a given hypothesis or theory?) And: What are its effects or consequences? (Or: How does it affect other phenomena?)

For example, depending upon the particular course, one might ask such questions as:

What were the causes of the American Revolution? What were its immediate consequences? Its long-range effects? (History)

What are the philosophical and historical sources of the concept of "individual rights?" What are the political consequences of different views of the nature of men's rights? (Government and Politics)

What are the major causes of inflation? What are its effects on the individual citizen? (Economics)

What forces led to the establishment of the field of Personnel Administration? In what ways have these developments affected business practices over the past several decades? (Business Administration)

What are some of the causal factors in schizophrenia? How does this disease affect the individual's ability to function? Can it be cured? How? (Psychology)

These examples could be multiplied indefinitely. Such questions require integrative reading because a great number of specific facts and concepts have to be brought together and logically organized before they can be answered.

Not all cause and effect questions are as complex as those just given. Simple cause and effect relationships are sometimes discussed in one or two paragraphs of a single article (e.g., Vitamin C and its alleged power to reduce the frequency of colds).

Implications   To imply means to suggest by logical necessity. In logic, statements of implication are often of the form "If X, then Y." In many texts the writer may give the "X" part but may leave it up to you to provide the "Y." Often this is because the implications are obvious. For example, if it were found that root beer were poisonous in the long run, what implications would this have for bottle manufacturers? for ginger-ale producers? for the vending machine business?

Other implications are left unstated because they are not obvious (even to the person who is writing). For instance, what would be the implications of the view that man has no individual rights but exists only to serve the State? Or suppose that you were told that man was completely determined by forces outside his control; that he had no choice about anything he believed, or thought, or did; that he was the helpless victim of all the different forces impinging upon him. What would be the implication of this view for your own life, if you accepted it? You might conclude such things as the following: "Why put forth any effort or plan for the future since the outcome of everything is predetermined anyway?" "If I commit a crime, I cannot be held responsible for it, since I could not help it." "Why read this book, since my grades are determined by forces I cannot control?"

One additional reason that implications may not be stated is that they are too numerous to mention in the context of a single article or chapter. Thus the burden of identifying them is placed mainly on the reader.

It is not only to meet course requirements that you need to read for implications. What you are taught in many college courses (e.g., economics, psychology, politics and government, and philosophy) may have significant implications for your own personal life and actions; thus it is worth identifying such implications explicitly.

Applications   The concept of application is related to that of implication, in that an application can be viewed as a putting-into-action or a putting-to-use of an implication. For example, one *implication* of the view that man cannot help or control any action he takes is that punishing men for their crimes is unjust, since they cannot help committing them. One *application* of this idea would be to abolish prisons. (And what are the implications of *that* idea for the average citizen, e.g., increased crime?) To take another example, how could one apply the discovery that giving a child early sensory and intellectual stimulation increases his intelligence? (One could apply it to the rearing of one's own children and in the design of nursery schools.) Not all applications are obvious since they presuppose the prior identification of an implication. But thinking about how an idea might be applied will help you to grasp its meaning more fully.

Critical Evaluation   Critical evaluation involves analyzing the theories, ideas, and conclusions you encounter in your reading with the attitude: "Does this make sense?" "Are the conclusions logically justified?" "Is there enough evidence?" "Does this contradict other evidence?"

There are several reasons why it is important to make critical evaluations of what you read. First, it is unfortunate but true (as you will discover for yourself) that some of the ideas you will be taught in college will be arbitrary, self-contradictory, or just plain nonsense. Thus you will want to protect yourself against naively accepting these wrong ideas. (This does not mean that you should gratuitously announce your personal views on every exam; only state your personal views on a test if they are asked for). It is important not to assume that something is true just because a teacher says it is true, or because it is written in a textbook. Always reserve judgment until you know the evidence and logical arguments (if any) behind the conclusions and assertions you encounter. In short, you must approach your college courses critically. Critically does not mean *cynically*, that is, with the idea that nothing is true, or important, or worthwhile. Reading critically means reading with the attitude that you will not accept anything as true until it is proven true by evidence and logical argument.

A second reason for reading critically is that college teachers sometimes ask for critical evaluations of your reading on tests or papers.

Third, critical reading helps to keep you *personally involved* in your assignments. In addition to the mental set of "What did X say," it gives you the additional mental set, "Does this make sense to me? Why or why not?"

Reading with a critical attitude will help the student to understand what he is reading, because it will help him to integrate it with his other beliefs and knowledge.

Critical reading basically involves the identification of *contradictions*, that is, implications or assertions or conclusions which are incompatible with each other or with the evidence given. If two propositions, statements, or assertions contradict each other, at least one of them must be wrong. For example, your mother cannot simultaneously be in New York and Los Angeles. Two plus 2 cannot equal both 4 and 5.

You may find contradictions, for example, between two different books on the same topic, or between textbook and lecture material, or between your prior knowledge and what you are taught in a course, between two different teachers or theorists, or between some theory and evidence which the theorist ignored, etc.

Consider another example. Suppose you were told that the total population of the United States was 138 people. You would have no trouble identifying the fact that this assertion contradicts *all* of your other knowledge about the population of the United States (statements in numerous books, published census figures, newspaper reports, attendance figures at sports events, the number of your personal acquaintances, etc.). It is doubtful that you will be offered anything this absurd in your college courses, but you might be offered something like the following in a college philosophy course: "You can't be certain of anything, that's for sure." (Contradiction: How can you be sure, if you can't be certain of anything?) Or: "Reason is only useful if man is infallible; man is not infallible since he makes mistakes; therefore, reason is useless." (Contradiction: A process of reasoning, specifically of logical deduction, was used to arrive at the conclusion that reason is useless.)

Not all contradictions will be this subtle. Often they will simply involve two theories which openly disagree. You may not have enough knowledge to take sides rationally in such cases, but you can at least identify that there is a disagreement and the nature of that disagreement (e.g., "Freud claims neurosis is caused by unconscious conflicts, whereas Skinner claims it is due to conditioning by one's environment").

Common Errors in Integrative Reading

You should watch for four common errors when doing integrative reading.

Subjectivism   This error, discussed in the previous chapter, also applies here. A student once came to my office complaining that he could not understand why he got such a low grade on a recent exam, since he had made all kinds of integrations with the material. When questioned closely about what kinds of integrations he had made, he acknowledged that they had been largely *personal* recategorizations based on his own interests and preferences rather than on an objective analysis of the material itself. Always distinguish clearly between your own views and those of the writer you are studying.

Nonessentials   Sometimes students analyze similarities and differences and recategorize based on inconsequential or trivial similarities and differences among ideas or phenomena (see footnote 2). For example, a zoological category named "crawling things" would not be very useful since it would put insects and babies in the same category.

Overdoing It   The student should not get so bogged down in integrations that he loses track of the actual content of the material he is reading. Remember that the type and amount of integrating you do should depend on your purpose, including the nature of your course requirements.

Holding Them in Your Head   Integrations held only in the head are likely to be both less clear and more easily forgotten than ones that are written down (in a notebook, in the margin of your book, etc.). It will be left to the reader to discover the implications and applications of this point! (See also Chapter 5.)

The Problem of Time

Like abstract reading, abstract integrative reading takes considerably more time than concrete-bound reading. It also takes more time than abstract reading since more connections are being made in integrative reading. However, the same arguments apply as were made in the previous chapter in defense of abstract reading. First, you can and should be selective about your integrative reading depending upon the nature of the course and the type of assignment. As stated in Chapter 2, you need to do proportionately more integrative reading in preparation for a paper or an all-essay exam than for a multiple-choice test or for short identification questions. Second, integrative reading is the only way to attain sufficient understanding for some types of tests or assignments. Third, you can expect integrative reading to become faster and more efficient with practice.

Summary

Abstract integrative reading is the highest level of reading. It entails making logical connections among the ideas and concepts you encounter. Specific types of integrations include: identifying similarities and differences; categorizing or recategorizing; identifying cause-effect relationships, implications, applications, and contradictions. The amount and types of integrations made will depend upon the reader's purpose. Common errors such as subjectivism, using nonessentials, overintegrating, and holding integrations only in the head should be avoided.

EXERCISES

1. Study the following selection carefully, looking for characteristics which could be compared. Then note (a) *similarities* and (b) *differences* between the three types of English colonies in America. A useful method would be to identify the main characteristics of each region (use subregions for the South, where relevant). In a space marked *similarities* list characteristics which two or more regions had in common (note which regions). In a space designated for *differences* list characteristics which were different for two or more regions (note which regions).

> **The English Colonies** By the middle of the eighteenth century three types of colonies had developed—northern, middle, and southern—with the Hudson River and the Mason-Dixon line the approximate dividing points.
>
> New England was a land of rocky soil, small farms, and independent towns. The business of each town was carried on by a town meeting, the purest form of democracy since the Athenian ecclesia, but true democracy did not exist because the Congregational Church dominated the political as well as the religious scene. Since the land was hilly and stony, the farms were small. Farmers had to clear off the stones before the land could be plowed. They piled the stones one on top of another to form walls around the fields. Many New Englanders turned to the sea for a living. The irregular coast line with its many bays and river mouths offered good harbors for fishing fleets. The magnificent pines and oaks of Maine

and New Hampshire provided the lumber for hundreds of ships built in harbors such as Portsmouth and Newport along the coast. When these ships took to the sea, they returned loaded with molasses from the Indies, fish from the Grand Banks, and flour from New York. . . .

The more fruitful soil of the middle colonies made this section the breadbasket of the colonies, and the Hudson River estates soon rivalled those in the South. Before long the ports of New York and Philadelphia, which exported the grain, had outstripped even Boston. New York and Pennsylvania also had the most important iron industries in the colonies. No one church dominated the middle colonies, nor were the inhabitants primarily English as in New England. More non-English elements lived in New York, New Jersey, and Pennsylvania than in the other colonies, with the Germans, Dutch, and Scotch-Irish the most important.

In the South the Anglican Church was established, but it did not control politics as the Congregational Church in New England. County government rather than the town system was in vogue. Tobacco, rice, and indigo plantations along the seacoast supplied products to export, but there were in addition many small, self-sufficient farms. The first slaves came to Virginia in 1619, and from then on slavery was an important part of the economy of the South. The interior of the early South differed from the seacoast in many ways —the farms were smaller, slavery was less common, and there was a higher proportion of non-English settlers. Land speculation and fur trading with the Indians were ways in which people from the coastal areas could make money in the interior.

D. Cole, *Atlas of American History* (New York: Ginn, 1963), p. 13.

2. The following is for an exercise in categorizing ideas. The categories and subcategories are not given by the author, nor are they

implied by paragraphing. This selection was *deliberately* written in a disorganized form, to provide the student with practice in *forming* categories and in *organizing* the material within the categories. Begin by finding the broadest category(s), then the next broadest (i.e., the subcategories); group the latter in the appropriate broad category. Then organize any relevant, specific facts under their appropriate subcategories in the proper order.

> An infant develops many skills from the time he is born. One skill related to the development of eye-hand coordination is the ability to follow a moving target as it passes overhead. The next big step in this chain is the infant's discovery of his hands. Another big development for the infant and toddler is the acquisition of language, a process which starts when he coos, mostly vowel sounds such as "ohh." Soon infants learn to imitate sounds, providing they already can make such sounds by themselves. Before long they are able to utter consonants and syllables such as "ba." One important milestone occurs when the baby swipes at objects with a closed fist. Another is listening to familiar words he hears spoken around him. Soon he can hold an object in his hand while looking at it, and finally he acquires the vital skill of looking at something and deliberately reaching for it (and grabbing it).
>
> A parent really begins to feel he can communicate with his child when he gives a simple command, and the child understands. This precedes the child's development of the ability to say numerous words.

3. In the following selection look for (a) *cause and effect relationships*; look also for (b) *implications* and *applications*. (You might want to review the relevant sections in the text before completing this exercise). Make written notes of your integrations.

> No virgin soil has ever been found to contain all the essential minerals in amounts now known to be somewhere near optimum in producing the health of plants, animals, or humans. Experiments

are carried on in which land is rebuilt with minerals and humus; the protein content of alfalfa
grown on such land has already been increased
from the average of 9 per cent to 32 per cent. The
protein content of other foods is increased correspondingly. No one yet knows the upper limit.
The quantities of the cobalt, copper, and other
trace minerals can be multiplied in our foods, yet
they never reach the point of toxicity. Plants
grown on such soil stay healthy, free from the doz-
ens of diseases which have changed agricultural
journals into medical magazines and treatises on
poison sprays.

Quotation reported in A. Davis, *Let's Eat Right to Keep
Fit* (New York: Harcourt Brace Jovanovich, 1970), p.
205.

4. In reading the following, practice critical evaluation. In this selection look for internal evidence to support conclusions, and consider
whether the ideas contradict other knowledge which you hold.

Certainly I believe in magic. I saw a magician
operating with an empty hat. He said "abracadabra," and a rabbit appeared. I carefully
noted that the only difference between the hat
empty and the hat filled with a rabbit was the
utterance of the magic formula.

L. Ruby, *Logic: An Introduction* (New York: Lippincott, 1960), p. 430.

5. For this selection, write your critical evaluation. (Note: This is a
satire.)

From the Manufacturers of Candles, Tapers,
Lanterns, Candlesticks, Street Lamps, Snuffers,
and Extinguishers, and from the Producers of Tal-
low, Oil, Resin, Alcohol, and Generally of Everything Connected with Lighting. . . .
We are suffering from the ruinous competition
of a foreign rival who apparently works under
conditions so far superior to our own for the pro-

duction of light that he is *flooding* the *domestic market* with it at an incredibly low price; for the moment he appears, our sales cease, all the consumers turn to him, and a branch of French industry whose ramifications are innumerable is all at once reduced to complete stagnation. This rival, which is none other than the sun, is waging war on us so mercilessly that we suspect he is being stirred up against us by perfidious . . . [England]. . . .

We ask you to be so good as to pass a law requiring the closing of all windows, dormers, skylights, inside and outside shutters, curtains, casements, . . . and blinds—in short, all openings, holes, chinks, and fissures through which the light of the sun is wont to enter houses, to the detriment of the fair industries with which, we are proud to say, we have endowed the country, a country that cannot, without betraying ingratitude, abandon us today to so unequal a combat.

From "A Petition" by F. Bastiat, in F. Bastiat, *Economic Sophisms* (Princeton: Van Nostrand, 1964), pp. 56–57; originally published in the 1850s.

Evaluating Your Answers

1. The following are valid examples of similarities and differences:

   a. *Similarities*
      —The middle colonies and the coastal South had many large farms.
      —New England and the inland South had small farms.
      —The middle colonies and the inland South had many non-English settlers.
      —New England and the middle colonies had thriving ports.
   b. *Differences*
      —The middle colonies and the coastal South had more large farms than New England.
      —The Congregational Church was dominant in New England, the Anglican church was the most established

church in the South, and no church was dominant in the middle colonies.

—The Congregational Church controlled politics in New England, but the Anglican Church did not control Southern politics.

—Towns were the main unit of government in New England, counties in the South.

—Fishing, shipbuilding, and shipping were important industries in New England; grain and iron production in the middle colonies; tobacco, rice, and indigo production plus fur trading in the South.

—More non-English inhabitants lived in the middle colonies and the Southern interior.

2. The following is the correct classification of the ideas in the selection. The specific facts should be listed in the order indicated.

Infant Skill Development
A. Eye-hand coordination
—Follows a moving target
—Discovers hands
—Swipes at objects
—Holds object and views it
—Masters visually directed reaching
B. Language
—Coos (vowel sounds)
—Imitates sounds he can already make
—Says syllables with consonants ("ba")
—Listens to familiar words
—Understands simple commands
—Says many words

3. The following are examples of acceptable answers:

a. *Cause and effect relationships*
—Fertilizing land enriches the food value of plants and makes them less susceptible to disease.
—Agricultural journals have become very concerned with diseases (and poison sprays) because plants are often not healthy.

b. *Implications and applications*
—Scientists might someday be able to control protein and mineral levels in crops.
—Farmers could get more plant protein and mineral yield per unit of land by adding minerals and humus.

—Some farmers might therefore be out of work unless demand increased.

—Soil *can* be improved.

—Protein is good for us.

—If the fertilizers were used more, many people in the world would benefit from increased plant protein yield per unit of land, since there is much starvation caused by protein deficiency.

—If fertilizers were used more, people in the fertilizer industry would have more work than at present.

—As a result feed grains might become less expensive, and so might meat.

—Increased plant protein might reduce the demand for meat.

—Experiments could be done, concerning the amounts and kinds of minerals to add to soil, and concerning the effects of insects on very healthy plants versus less healthy ones.

4. For an acceptable critical evaluation, a student might write:

This statement contradicts my knowledge about material objects; specifically, they don't appear "from nowhere." Furthermore, the person allegedly writing the paragraph does not actually cite evidence to support his assertion that *nothing* else was done by the magician except to say, "abracadabra." He merely says he "carefully noted . . ." and it is not clear that he actually examined each hat thoroughly.

A person writing the foregoing evaluation would be considering major issues involved in a critical evaluation: Is a writer noncontradictory, and does he offer evidence to support his conclusion(s)?

5. A good answer would be the following:

The Manufacturers and Producers are contradicting themselves; they want to *force* people to block out the sun, yet they want the freedom to do business as they wish. In addition, the sun could not have inundated their market since the sun was shining before they began manufacturing candles.

Furthermore, the petition overlooks the fact that when circumstances make it unnecessary to manufacture a commodity, those workers are available to spend their energy creating some other product of value.

Finally, no evidence is given to prove that England is responsible for sunlight in France.

Here is an example of a poor answer:

I like the sun and feel that it is a joy to have it there. It's nicer to see and use the sun than artificial lighting. The sun is natural. I don't think the sun comes out enough. They just want sun to go away so they will make more money.

This answer is purely subjective and does not evaluate the logical validity or the objectivity of the selection.

5. How To Identify and Designate What Is Important

All reading is selective, even the reading of the most carefully written and edited textbooks. There are two basic reasons for this: (1) all reading is done with an explicit or implicit purpose; thus some of the material will be more relevant to this purpose than other material; and (2) some parts of any given selection are objectively more important than others; for example, all books contain "filler material" such as transition statements that connect one paragraph to another (e.g., "Now let us discuss another aspect of the Constitution," etc.) which are not important in themselves.

One of the most crucial skills a good student must acquire is that of distinguishing important from unimportant material, or more precisely, distinguishing among various degrees of importance. The reason for making such distinctions is that the more important content can be singled out for special study and emphasis while the less important material can be ignored or studied less. Singling out what is important also helps the student to organize the material in his own mind, that is, to form categories based on relevant similarities and differences (see Chapter 4).

Identifying What Is Important

How can the student decide what is important and what is not? There are two main sources of clues: those in the book itself and those outside the book.

Clues in the Book Itself   Many clues as to what is important come from the book itself, especially if the book is a textbook. Below is a list of clues which the student should look for in his reading material. Not all books will have all of these, but all books will have some of them:

—Topics listed in the Table of Contents or in an Abstract at the beginning of the chapter or article.

—Chapter, section, and paragraph titles or headings (usually given in boldface type).

—Topic sentences. Well-written paragraphs have a topic sentence (often but not always the first sentence) which states the central idea of the paragraph.

—Numbered or lettered lists (e.g., "There are three types of cells; one type is . . .").

—Italicized terms or concepts.

—All types of classifications (e.g., "There are several different approaches to the study of man: the Freudian, the Behavioristic, and the Humanistic . . .").

—Lists of the causes and/or the effects of a phenomenon.

—Specific theories associated with an individual whose name is mentioned (e.g., "Adler's theory of personality revolves around the concept of striving for superiority," etc.).

—New concepts, that is, concepts not encountered before in the book and which the book introduces, defines, and/or explains.

—Specific discoveries or research findings reported in the book.

—Graphs, tables, charts, and diagrams.

—Formulas, especially in the physical sciences (e.g., mathematics, and engineering).

—Topics to which a large amount of space is devoted.

—General conclusions reached about some topic. (The student should, of course, know the basis for these conclusions.)

—Concepts which are needed to solve problems, to complete exercises, or to discuss topics given at the end of a chapter.

—Terms and definitions listed in the index or the glossary at the end of a chapter or book.

Clues from Outside the Book   This category of clues would include:
—The title and description of the course for which the book is read (see course catalogue).
—Specific statements made by the course instructor or inferences made from his statements. Such statements are quite important and should be supplemented whenever possible by direct questions addressed to the professor regarding what he expects the students to know.
—Past examinations in the course, *if* these are available and *if* the past exams were given by the same instructor and/or were on the same text. If past exams are not available, the student can talk to other students who previously had the professor in that course.
—Once the course has begun, the student can use exams from the course itself as a basis for future studying. Past exams do not, of course, tell the student what specific questions will be asked on future exams, but they may reveal the *type* of question the instructor likes to ask.
—Individual conferences with the course instructor.
—Handouts from the instructor concerning course themes, etc.

After deciding what is or is not important, or what is more and what is less important, the student needs to have some method of designating this material for the purpose of later review. Let us now discuss how this may be done.

Designating What Is Important

There are two basic ways to indicate what is important: underlining and note-taking. Each method has advantages and disadvantages, although, as will be seen, the benefits of both methods may be attained by combining them.

Underlining   The basic advantages of underlining are: (1) it is quick; (2) it keeps the material in its original context; and (3) it allows one to discover errors easily; for example, if during an earlier reading one neglected to underline an important point, one has a chance of catching it the next time the passage is read.

On the other hand, underlining has drawbacks. It discourages reformulating the concepts in your own words, a process which is helpful in understanding (see Chapter 3). Further, underlining is often done passively and mechanically with little thought being given to the meaning of the material being read. Some students use underlining as a substitute for understanding instead of as a supplement to it.

The student who chooses to use underlining should be aware of its possible drawbacks and should also understand the general rules of underlining described below.

How much to underline.   The purpose of underlining is to reduce the amount of material to be restudied for exams (as well as to indicate the appropriate degree of emphasis to be given to various parts of the material). Thus if one underlines everything, one might as well underline nothing. On the other hand, if one underlines almost nothing, it will not be of much help either. As a rough estimate, the student should underline somewhere between 20 percent and 50 percent of a typical textbook. Figures outside this range might be appropriate with some texts, with other types of books (e.g., novels) or with particular parts of chapters or books.

It is not necessary to underline every word, even in an important sentence. Indicating the key words or key phrases within a sentence will often suffice.

When to underline.   The basic principle to observe here is that underlining should *follow* and not precede understanding. There is no way to know what is important until one has at least some idea of what the writer is saying. This does not mean, as asserted in some study-skill texts, that one should always read a chapter all the way through for understanding and then go back and reread it for the purpose of underlining. One could just as well do both on a paragraph-by-paragraph or section-by-section basis. This can be left to the discretion of the student.

The student must be strongly cautioned not to confuse the process of underlining with the process of understanding. *Underlining as such is drawing lines and nothing more.* Do not assume that the motions of underlining guarantee understanding. The temptation to underline *passively* is greatly reduced when underlining is postponed until after at least some understanding has been achieved. A recent study demonstrated that active underlining or highlighting (i.e., underlining accompanied by active reading) produced significantly more learning than *passive* highlighting (i.e., underlining without active reading).[1]

How to mark the book.   As an alternative to literal underlining (which should be done with a ruler and a dark pencil or a pen), some

1.   R. L. Fowler and A. S. Barker, "Effectiveness of Highlighting for Retention of Text Material," *Journal of Applied Psychology*, 59 (1974), 358–64.

students use "highlighting," which involves running a colored but transparent felt-tip marker through the words and phrases to be stressed. Yellow is a useful color because it contrasts well with the black print and is highly transparent. Brackets or vertical lines in the margins can also be used as a means of emphasis.

It is strongly suggested that the student have a method of indicating *different degrees of importance,* since all underlined material is not of equal significance. One could, for instance, use highlighting for the most important material and underlining for the next most important. Or highlighting could be done in two different colors (e.g., yellow and green). Or one could use underlining plus brackets in the margins. The student should be able to indicate at least *two* degrees of importance with whatever system he uses. Some students use three degrees, but any more than this may lead to confusion.

Note-taking

Comprehensive note-taking. When a student thinks of note-taking, he often thinks of notes that are so detailed that they can be used to study for an exam without further reference to the text. Such *comprehensive* notes have several disadvantages, which are the opposite of the advantages of underlining just described: (1) making such notes is very time-consuming; (2) notes require taking the material out of its original context, which may distort its meaning; and (3) there is no chance to catch errors of omission unless one goes back to the original text—a procedure which consumes even more time and which contradicts the main purpose of comprehensive note-taking, which is to avoid having to reread the text.

On the other hand, note-taking does get the student actively involved in the material and facilitates understanding by encouraging the student to reformulate and recategorize the concepts.

Is there any method of note-taking which retains at least some of its advantages while avoiding its major drawbacks?

Working notes. The idea of "working notes" has been suggested by one study-skills expert as a solution to this problem.[2] To construct working notes, the student jots down only phrases indicative of the main points (terms, ideas) and subpoints, each subpoint being under its proper heading. The result is a page or half-page outline of each chapter that helps to organize the material in the student's mind and to guide him in his review. Such notes supplement rather than replace underlining as described above. Preliminary evidence indicates that *after about a month's practice,* students find measurable

2. F. P. Robinson, *Effective Study* (New York: Harper & Row, 1970), p. 23.

benefits occurring as a result of using this technique (see footnote 2).

Notes in the margins.   The student can also make notations in the margin of his text as an aid to both emphasis and understanding. These notations may include:

—Questions, such as those formed by rewording the headings (see Chapter 3).
—Brief reformulations of (some of) the ideas or concepts in one's own words.
—Brief integrations with related materials (e.g., lectures, other material in the same chapter or book, etc.).
—Numbers and letters to indicate lists of facts, reasons, conclusions, similarities, etc. and the organization of categories and subcategories.
—Question marks to indicate a passage that is unclear and requires further study or a word that needs to be looked up.
—Symbols to indicate that the instructor has explicitly stated that a concept, passage, or section be given careful study.

Combining Underlining, Note-taking, and Notes in the Margin

This writer recommends underlining combined with working notes and notations in the margins as giving the best combination of speed, understanding, and organization. The working notes can be used, before the material is reread, as a survey of the material to be covered and as a basis for *reprogramming* one's mind with the proper mental orders (see Chapter 3). They can also be used for the purpose of testing one's recall (see Chapters 6 and 7). In addition they can be used to prepare for exams (see Chapter 12). The underlining will tell one how much attention to give to each part of the text when reviewing (for example, nonunderlined passages need only be skimmed). The notations in the margin will remind one of the integrations one has previously made and inform one of any further work that needs to be done (as in the case of a question mark indicating the need for further study).

These ideas are illustrated in Figures 1 and 2 below. Figure 1 contains a passage from the writing of sociologist Max Weber. It has been underlined in accordance with the principles noted above, using straight underlining for the most important points and brackets for the next most important points. Notes in the margins summarize and integrate the main points. Figure 2 contains working notes made from the same passage.

Figure 1. Sample Passage with Underlining and Notes in Margins

VIII. BUREAUCRACY

I: Characteristics of Bureaucracy   Modern official-dom functions in the following specific manner:

I. There is the principle of fixed and official jurisdictional areas, which are generally ordered by rules, that is, by laws or administrative regulations.

1. The regular activities required for the purposes of the bureaucratically governed structure are distributed in a fixed way as official duties.

2. The authority to give the commands required for the discharge of these duties is (distributed in a stable way) and is strictly delimited by rules concerning the coercive means, physical, sacerdotal, or otherwise, which may be placed at the disposal of officials.

3. Methodical provision is made for the regular and continuous fulfillment of these duties and (for the execution of the corresponding rights;) only persons who have the generally regulated qualifications to serve are employed. . . .

II. The principles of office hierarchy and of levels of graded authority mean (a firmly ordered system of super- and subordination in which there is a supervision of the lower offices by the higher ones.) Such a system offers the governed the possibility of appealing the decision of a lower office to its higher authority, (in a definitely regulated manner.) With the full development of the bureaucratic type, the office hierarchy is (mono-cratically) organized. The principle of hierarchical office authority is found in all bureaucratic structures: in state and ecclesiastical structures as well as large party organizations and private enterprises. . . .

III. The management of the modern office is based upon written documents ("the files"), which are preserved in their original or draught

Margin notes:

① Jurisdiction fixed by rules and regulations

a) duties

b) authority limited ?

c) qualifications

② Hierarchy (appeal)

? all types of bureaucracy

③ Written documents

implies bureaucracy is objective — is this true?

how differ from other types of authority?

Figure 1 (Continued)

? — form. There is, therefore,(a staff of(subaltern)offi-
cials and(scribes) of all sorts.)The body of officials
actively engaged in a "public" office, along with
the respective apparatus of material implements
and the files, make up a("bureau.")(In private en-
terprise, the "bureau" is often called "the office.")

are there also differences between public and private organizations —?

Max Weber, "Bureaucracy," in *From Max Weber: Essays in Sociology*, ed. H. H. Gerth and C. Wright Mills (New York: Galaxy, Oxford University Press, 1958), pp. 196–97.

Figure 2. "Working Notes" on Passage in Figure 1

Bureaucracy

I. Characteristics
1. Fixed jurisdiction by rules, laws, regulations about:
   a. official duties
   b. limits of authority
   c. duties fulfilled by qualified persons
2. Hierarchy of authority (possibility of appeal)
3. Use of written documents (files)
   the bureau
   the office

Note that in the left-hand margin of the selection is a summary of the basic ideas of the passage. These are expanded slightly in the Working Notes. Observe also that the main categories and sub-categories are identified with appropriate numbers and letters.

The right-hand margin contains integrative questions that occurred to me as I read the passage. The same integrative questions would not, of course, occur to every reader. Nor are such questions always necessary if all that is required in the course is abstract reading.

The single question marks connected to the circled words in both margins indicate words that may need to be looked up in a dictionary. Technical terms, of course, may not always be found in a standard dictionary, but their meaning will sometimes be given in other parts of the text or can be inferred from the context in which they appear.

Summary

All reading is selective. The student can determine what is more and what is less important by factors in the text itself such as boldface headings and italicized terms and by factors outside the text such as teacher's comments. The student should designate what is important by means of underlining, working notes, and notations in the margins of the book. These provide a guide and a framework in which to reread the material and to prepare for exams. (The student should be careful not to confuse underlining with understanding.)

EXERCISES

1. Read the following selection and designate what is important in the passage. Use a system of underlining, highlighting, and/or bracketing that shows at least *two* degrees of importance. You should also make some notes in the margins and should indicate (with letters and/or numbers) how the concepts are classified. Before you underline (or bracket) indicate your system below.

_____ designation to be used for items of most importance

_____   designation to be used for items of
                                   secondary importance

_____   designation to be used for items of
                                   less importance (optional)

The Origin of Root Systems   When a seed germi-
nates, the first root arises from the lower end, or
radicle, of the embryo plant and grows downward
into the soil. This first root is the *primary root.*
After a short period of growth, the primary root
produces lateral branches, or *secondary roots.* . . .
Further branching of secondary roots occurs as the
plant develops its entire root system. . . .
Types of Roots and Root Systems   If a primary root
continues to grow and remains the major root of
the system, it is known as a *taproot.* Plants with
taproots have many advantages. A long taproot is
ideal for anchorage. Taproots also reach water
supplies deep in the ground. The alfalfa, for example, has a taproot fifteen feet or more in length.
This explains why fields of alfalfa remain green
during dry periods when shallow-rooted grasses
turn yellow and brown. Long taproots also account for oak and hickory forests on dry hillsides
and ridges. The taproots of many plants become
thick and fleshy and serve as underground
storehouses for the food supply of the plant. We
grow certain of these plants, including the beet,
radish, carrot, turnip, and parsnip, as root crops.
    In many plants, including the grasses, the
growth of the primary root is rapidly surpassed by
the growth of its branches, or secondary roots.
Roots of this kind are *fibrous roots.* Fibrous root
systems are usually shallow and spread through a
large area of soil. They are efficient organs of
water and mineral absorption. Fibrous roots are
also important as soil binders, anchoring soil particles and preventing erosion by water and wind.

J. Otto and A. Towle, *Modern Biology* (New York: Holt,
Rinehart and Winston, 1969), pp. 335–36.

Now check your work for the following:

—Did you underline between 20 percent and 50 percent of the passage?

—Did you designate different degrees of importance?

—Did you underline *all* of the main headings?

—Did you designate the main headings or terms and their definitions as being *equally* important?

—Did you designate the examples of the concepts (or additional details) as being *less* important than the abstract definitions? (Doing otherwise would imply that you were doing concrete-bound reading).

—Did you indicate, in addition to your underlining, how the ideas were classified (e.g., by numbering or lettering main categories and subcategories)?

2. Now that you have read and studied the above passage, construct "working notes" from it. (Look back at the passage as much as you wish). Your underlining and notes in the margin should help you. Indicate which are main categories and which are subcategories.

Evaluating Your Answers

1. In the following example, items of most importance are underlined with a double line, those of secondary importance with a single line, and those of less importance are bracketed. *Definitions* of concepts and their *names* are generally given *equal* emphasis. (Many students tend to mark names or terms as being more important than their definitions, which might lead them to ignore these definitions when they review the material.) In addition to the underlining and bracketing, notes in the left margin are used to summarize the salient points and to indicate the major categories and subcategories.

The notes in the right-hand margin indicate the reason why certain terms or phrases were underlined. These notes are *not* the type which you should be making. They are simply to explain the reasons for *our* underlinings.

The Origin Ⓐ of Root Systems When a seed germinates, the first root arises (from the lower end, or *radicle*, of the embryo plant) and grows downward into the soil. This first root is the *primary root*.	Heading Italicized new concepts and definitions

After a short period of growth, the primary root produces lateral branches, or *secondary roots*. . . . Further branching of secondary roots occurs as the plant develops its entire root system. . . .

Types of Roots and Root Systems If a primary root continues to grow and remains the major root of the system, it is known as a *taproot*. Plants with taproots have many advantages. A long taproot is ideal for anchorage. Taproots also reach water supplies deep in the ground. The alfalfa, for example, has a taproot fifteen feet or more in length. This explains why fields of alfalfa remain green during dry periods when shallow-rooted grasses turn yellow and brown. Long taproots also account for oak and hickory forests on dry hillsides and ridges. The taproots of many plants become thick and fleshy and serve as underground storehouses for the food supply of the plant. We grow certain of these plants, including the beet, radish, carrot, turnip, and parsnip, as root crops.

In many plants, including the grasses, the growth of the primary root is rapidly surpassed by the growth of its branches, or secondary roots. Roots of this kind are *fibrous roots*. Fibrous root systems are usually shallow and spread through a large area of soil. They are efficient organs of water and mineral absorption. Fibrous roots are also important as soil binders, anchoring soil particles and preventing erosion by water and wind.

Margin notes (left):
① taproot (primary)
② fibrous root (secondary)

advantages of taproot:
-anchorage
-reach deep water
-store food

advantages of fibrous roots:
-good water & mineral absorption
-soil binders

Margin labels (right):
Heading
Italicized new concep and definitic
List
Italicized new concept and definitio
List

2. The following is an example of a good set of working notes. The main terms (with brief descriptions of some) are given, and the concepts are classified:

I. Root systems
   A. Origin
      1. Primary root (first to emerge)
      2. Secondary roots
   B. Types
      1. Taproot (long, dominant, primary root)
      2. Fibrous roots (extensive, dominant, secondary roots)

The following are some examples of inadequate working notes:

I. Root systems
   A. Origin
      1. different roots
   B. Types
      1. descriptions

These working notes are useless because they contain too little information. Terms and brief descriptions should have been jotted down instead of "different roots" and "descriptions."

I. Root systems
   A. Primary root
   B. Secondary root
   C. Taproot
   D. Fibrous root

The foregoing are poor working notes because, in addition to being incomplete, the material is incorrectly classified. The items appear as *four different* types of root systems. However, taproots are primary roots, and fibrous roots are secondary roots; thus the above listing is misleading.

6. How To Program Your Memory: The Nature of Memory

Memory is the capacity to retain in awareness or to bring to awareness something you have been aware of previously. Picturing in your mind what your house looks like, recalling a fact or passage from a book you read a week ago, recognizing an old friend—these are all acts of memory.

Memory Versus Understanding

Many students complain of the need to "memorize" course material, claiming that "understanding it" should be sufficient. This view is partly right and partly wrong. It is right in that there *is* a distinction between understanding and memory. To understand something means to grasp its meaning (see Chapters 3 and 4). Memorization involves being able to pull material out of your subconscious mind (out of "storage," so to speak) on order. Since understanding and memorizing are different operations, it is possible to do one without the other. Thus you can memorize or learn to recite a list of word

sounds (such as a poem or a definition) without having any idea what the words mean. This is what people usually have in mind when they object to the practice of "rote memorization." And they are right to object to it, because memory without understanding *is* useless unless you want to hire yourself out as a trained parrot. However, one can also understand an idea or concept but not retain it in memory (or not retain it in such a way that it can be called out on order, when you need it).

Students who claim that understanding alone should be sufficient for college courses are mistaken for two reasons. First, you could not prove that you really understood a concept if you failed to retain that understanding long enough to answer a question about it on an exam. A second reason pertains to the function of memory in human life.

The Function of Memory

Memory enables you to retain over time the knowledge which you have acquired and thus enables you to use that knowledge to guide your choices and actions. Knowledge which you could not retain would be useless; in fact, it would not really be knowledge at all but just a momentary "flash" of insight that would be gone almost as soon as it arrived.

To consider the practical implications of this, imagine a doctor trying to perform an operation on a patient without being able to recall the basic facts of anatomy, physiology, and surgery. Picture a pilot who could not retain in his mind the location, function, and mode of operation of the controls trying to fly a plane. Imagine a professor who could not remember anything about the subject matter he was teaching trying to correct exams or answer students' questions. None of these actions could be performed unless the prerequisite knowledge was programmed into the surgeon's or the pilot's or the professor's memory. The same goes for any profession or any purposeful task that a human being performs.

Retaining one's knowledge in memory is an essential part of the act of learning. If you do not retain what you have learned, you have not really learned at all. *Learning in this context can be defined as understanding plus memory.* Thus the issue for the student should not be understanding *or* memory but rather understanding *and* memory—i.e., learning.

Some Characteristics of Memory

Memory Is Limited   Your capacity to remember or retain material is limited, that is, finite. There is only a certain amount of information a person can take in and retain in any given span of time. Individuals differ among themselves in this capacity but each person still has his own limit. (This capacity can, however, be increased with practice.)

The finite capacity of memory is the reason why the widely used technique known as "cramming" is not a very effective method of memorizing (or not nearly as effective as would be learning the same material more gradually). Cramming involves trying to program too much material into your memory at once, and thus most of it is not retained. (Much of it is forgotten before the exam, the rest right after.) Cramming is like trying to pour water through a funnel too fast; a lot gets lost in the process. Furthermore, the difficulties and frustrations involved in cramming can cause the student to become anxious and lose confidence in his ability.

The Pause That Impresses   The reason that your capacity for programming memory is limited is that such programming presupposes and depends on a sequence of mental processes, each of which requires a finite amount of time to occur. For example, perception requires a certain amount of time; understanding (including integrating) takes a certain amount of time; programming memory takes a certain amount of time. If you try to go too fast, your mind will simply not have time to perform all of these operations. The result will be that either some of the operations or some of the material will be skipped, and the result will be a failure to learn or incomplete learning.

It may help, as an antidote to the tendency to go too fast, to pause deliberately as you study to give the material time to "sink in" or "impress" itself on your mind. As an additional benefit, you may find that during these pauses relevant integrations can be made which will help to increase your understanding of the material. This is not to imply that learning is a passive process; on the contrary, it is a very active process (see Chapters 3, 4, 5, and 7). But it is a process which cannot be rushed.

Now is a good time to pause and think about what you have just read!

Minimizing Interference   Experts in the field of learning and memory have found that one reason forgetting occurs is that experiences which follow learning interfere with the earlier learning. The best way to prevent such interference (assuming the material has been thoroughly programmed to start with) is to *go to sleep* right after studying, since the state of sleep involves less mental activity than almost anything you do when waking. Of course, this is not always possible but it could be done the night before an important exam.

When To Program Memory   The experts suggest that you begin programming your memory *when you first begin reading* a given selection (that is, as soon as you have begun to understand it), rather than reading only for understanding the first time and then reading to program memory several weeks later (such as the night before the exam!). The reason is that if you start programming your memory right away, it will dramatically increase the amount recalled when you go back to the material later.[1] Thus you will have less to learn the week before the exam and you will know the material more thoroughly. Some experts suggest daily review of previously read course material, but unfortunately this is not always possible owing to time limitations.

Memory and Bias   Some students have a tendency to refuse to study, or to refuse to study thoroughly, material (theories, viewpoints, conclusions) with which they personally disagree. This might be defensible if your only reason for studying were your own personal enlightenment. However, when you are enrolled in a course, the instructor usually wants to know only whether or not you have learned the assigned material. Thus, in the context of studying for an exam, learning only what you agree with is a form of subjectivism (see Chapters 3 and 4) and should be avoided. Remember, you will not be "contaminated" by views you disagree with, so long as you make a clear distinction in your own mind between what the author or teacher says and what you consider to be true.

Rest   Programming memory is hard work. You may find that short rest periods after every half hour or hour or several hours of study (depending on your interest in the material and your capacity for concentration) will help. Such rest periods fulfill several functions: they reduce fatigue and dissipate boredom (see Chapter 15); they allow subconscious integrations to take place; they reduce interference; and they may even yield a fresh perspective on the material.

Memory an Acquired Skill   While there are individuals who seem to have been born with "photographic memories," for most of us the

1. W. Pauk, *How to Study in College* (Boston: Houghton Mifflin, 1962), pp. 75–76.

ability to remember is acquired through practice, just like all of our other skills. It involves identifying and learning to use specific techniques, i.e., to perform specific mental operations on the material to be remembered.

These operations are described in the next chapter.

Summary

Memory is the capacity to bring to or retain in awareness something you had previously been aware of. It is not the same as understanding but rather a supplement to understanding that allows you to retain your understanding over time, i.e., to learn. Several characteristics of memory should be recognized: memory is limited, therefore cramming should be avoided; momentary pauses during study will help allow the material to "sink in"; interference between new learning and later experiences may be minimized by going to sleep after studying. You should start programming your memory when you first begin to study rather than at the last minute; avoid programming only material you personally agree with; take short rest breaks as needed; and remember that programming memory is an acquired skill.

EXERCISES

1. Discuss the following: Why is cramming for an exam a poor idea? Give as many reasons as you can.

2. Explain the difference between and the relationship between memory and understanding.

Evaluating Your Answers

1. Cramming is a poor idea because:
   a. The amount one can memorize at a given time is limited. When cramming, a student probably would not pause during the studying to give his mind time to process the material.

   b. The difficulties encountered while cramming can lower one's confidence.

2. Understanding is tying (relating) new concepts or ideas to the rest of your knowledge. Memory is the ability to bring material out of your subconscious, on order, into conscious awareness. Memory enables you to retain and use the material you have understood. Without memory you could not learn.

7. How To Program Your Memory: Specific Techniques

Before describing techniques that will help you to program your memory, one method often used by students that will *not* help you very much should be mentioned. It is known as *passive rereading* or *passive repetition* and involves simply reading the material over and over again, with no specific purpose in mind and with little or no attempt to understand or integrate. (Passive rereading is by its nature concrete-bound or perceptual-level reading). If your mind is not performing any operations on the material you read, not performing them twenty times over is going to be of little help. Programming your memory, like understanding, is an active, not a passive process.

What techniques, then, are effective for this purpose?

Understanding and Active (Re-) Reading

In Chapter 6 it was stated that understanding and memory are separate functions and involve separate operations; that is, one can do each without the other. Understanding and memory are not entirely unrelated, however, since the mental processes which produce understanding, i.e., abstract and integrative reading, are themselves an aid to memory.

70

These two levels of reading are profoundly active types of reading in that they involve associating new ideas with "old" or previously learned facts or ideas. This process of tying the not-yet-known to the known makes the new ideas personally *meaningful*. The more familiar and meaningful a new idea becomes, the more easily it is recalled.

You can supplement your initial abstract and/or integrative reading with an active rereading of the assigned material, concentrating on the underlined portions. In addition to facilitating recall, this procedure may result in integrations which you did not think of during the first reading.

Establishing the Proper Mental Set: The Intent to Remember

Just as you need to program your mind with the proper orders in order to understand (see Chapter 3), you need to do the same in order to program your memory. The proper mental set in this case consists of establishing a standing order in your mind to the effect: "I am going to remember this." One way to emphasize this intention is to look up from the book occasionally and try to summarize what you have just read. Some students do this after each paragraph (once they have understood it), but it can be done with larger units as well. Try it with the next two paragraphs below.

In addition to a general intent to remember, you can program your mind with *specific purposes*, such as to recall the answers to the questions you posed after your initial survey (Chapter 3). When you complete a section or chapter, see if you can recall the answers to these questions. (You are cautioned not to set purposes which involve impossible memory feats such as, "I must remember every word." Memory, like other aspects of studying, must be selective.)

It must be stressed that an intention to remember does not consist of telling oneself, "Gee, I *hope* I remember this later." An intention is a *genuine determination* to take a certain action; it is not a half-hearted wish or feeling.

Now, what did the last two paragraphs say? Did having an intent to remember them help you to do so?

It is not fully known why having an intent to recall helps learning, but many experiments have shown that recall is better when there is a specific intent to remember than when remembering is incidental (not consciously intended).

To illustrate the point, see if you can, right now, correctly indicate the layout of a telephone dial (with the appropriate letters and numbers together) on Figure 3. (For the correct layout, consult any telephone. Touchtone phones involve the same letter-number combinations as dial phones.)

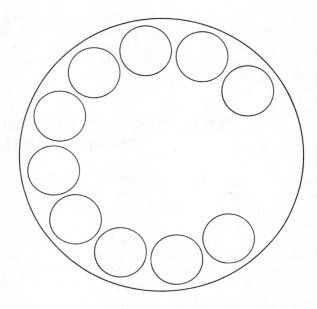

Figure 3

In my experience fewer than 5 students in 100 can do this without error, even though all of them have made hundreds or thousands of telephone calls during their lifetimes. Memorizing the layout of the dial, however, was always incidental to their making of the calls; thus little memorization took place. With a specific intent to remember, however, you could easily go to a phone right now and correctly memorize the layout in one or two minutes.

One reason why intentional programming is superior to incidental remembering has been identified through experimental research. Individuals who have an intention to recall perform *different mental operations* on the material they read than those with no such intention. Some of these operations are described below.

Rehearsal

This may be the single most useful method of programming memory, since it may be used with any type of material and is aimed directly and solely at this end. It consists of attempting to recall or reproduce the material (concepts, facts, definitions, ideas, theories, principles, etc.) *without looking at the material while you do it.*

For example, if you had a list of 20 French words to translate into English, you could cover the answers and go down the list over and over again, trying to translate each word without looking at the answers (except to see if your answer was correct). This method is preferable to passive rereading, because it demands of you exactly what a test demands of you, namely, producing the correct answers to a series of questions *without* the answers being visible. As you go over and over your list, you can make a special note of the concepts you missed repeatedly so that they can be set aside for extra study later.

While saying your answers out loud (recitation) is not necessary, it may help to keep you from going too fast and "slurring" over the answers. You could also have friends test you on the material and check your answers.

Your "working notes" (Chapter 5) can be used to guide your rehearsal, since, if constructed properly, they will contain all the major concepts and ideas in each chapter that you read. You could begin by going through your notes for each chapter and trying to recall the meaning of and identifying relevant facts about each item on your outline. If the test you are studying for will include essay questions, you should also test yourself for recall of the outline itself.

One important warning when using rehearsal or recitation: be careful of using too short a time-span when practicing recall. For example, you could go through each chapter as follows: look at the definition or description of the first major idea, cover it up with your hand, immediately recite it from memory; look at the description of the second major idea, cover it up, immediately recite it from memory, and so on throughout the chapter. While you could *begin* rehearsing with such a procedure, if that were all you did it would be insufficient, because you would be programming only *short-term* rather than the *long-term* memory which you need for a test. During a test you would not be allowed to follow the procedure just described. You would be required to hold *all* of the material in memory at once since you cannot look at your book once the test starts. Thus you must eventually be able to recall in units larger than individual ideas or terms (e.g., chapters) and over correspondingly longer time spans.

Mnemonic Devices

"Mnemonic" (pronounced "neemonik") means "assisting to memory"; thus mnemonic devices are aids or "tricks" that one can use to facilitate recall. The devices to be discussed in this category are most useful when the material to be programmed consists mainly of isolated facts, lists of concrete facts, or ideas which have no obvious logical sequence or interrelationship. While mnemonic devices cannot replace the methods described above, the student may encounter courses, or parts of courses, or specific types of material where the use of this method is both helpful and appropriate.[1]

There are a variety of mnemonic aids which you may find useful.

Mental Images   This device consists of forming a clear, vivid mental image or mental picture which can be easily associated with the object, or person, or term to be remembered.

For example, suppose one wanted to memorize the Morse code. One Boy Scout instructor (Raymond Teichman) developed a system that associated each letter with a word and each word with a picture. For instance, he said "c" stands for two (baseball) "caps," and the two caps together look like this: ___⌒\ ___⌒\, that is, like −.−. (dash-dot-dash-dot) which is the Morse symbol for the letter "c." To take another example, suppose that a person you had just met was named Richard Strayshoe, and you wanted to remember his name but had a great deal of trouble doing it. You might associate his first name with the word "rich" and the second with the words "stray" and "shoe." You could then form a mental image of a shoe (perhaps one of your own) wandering around (like a stray) in a pile of dollar bills (as though it were rich). If you could recall these images when you saw the person or thought about the person, you could very quickly come up with his correct name. Better yet if you can

---

1.   For a useful discussion of mnemonic devices, see G. H. Bower, "Educational Applications of Mnemonic Devices," in *Interaction: Readings in Human Psychology*, ed. K. O. Doyle (Lexington, Mass.: Heath, 1973), pp. 201–10.

associate some physical characteristic of the person with his name i.e., a tall person named Sue Pine or a stocky person named Bill Barrel).

Consider an example from a more academic context: suppose you had trouble recalling the meaning of "electroencephalogram" (a record of the electrical wave patterns given off by a person's brain). The abbreviation for this term is EEG; you might then picture an egg (which is almost like EEG) sitting on top of a person's head (perhaps being etched with wave patterns). Then when you were asked what an EEG was, you could, by recalling this image (an image of an egghead?), remember that it had to do with the brain, and specifically with brain wave patterns.

It is possible to develop whole strings of images which can help you to recall lists of words. For instance, take the following list: apple, head, television, truck, grass, river. If you picture in your mind, very clearly and vividly: an apple sitting on a person's head, the head sitting on top of a TV set, the TV set being carried by a truck, across a grassy field, which ends in a river—if you can picture this sequence, you will easily be able to recall this list of words. (Some people picture a room or house with each object in a specific location in it.)[2] There may not be too many courses where such lists are required, but if there are, you can easily see how you might go about programming such a list into memory. The method of forming mental images, is, of course, more appropriate for relatively concrete terms and words than it is for more abstract ideas and concepts.

You will recall that the use of mental images was advocated in Chapter 3 as an aid to understanding. Here they are also being suggested as an aid to memory. Can the same image be used for both? The answer is yes, if you wish. For example, in the case of the electroencephalogram (EEG), you could picture a person with an egg-shaped head with electrodes attached to it as an aid to both understanding and memory. However, you will not always have to do both. For example, you might need an image to understand a concept but not to recall it. Or you might understand a concept quite well but need an image to help recall certain details.

Words or Phrases Composed of Key Letters Suppose one wanted to program into memory the following six methods used in scientific investigation: observation; categorization (or conceptualization);

---

2. G. H. Bower, "Analysis of a Mnemonic Device," *American Scientist* 58 (September–October 1970), 496–510.

reasoning (deduction, induction, etc.); hypothesis formation; measurement; and experimentation. Assume that you had grasped the abstract meaning of and were able to explain each of these concepts but had trouble remembering the full list of six methods. You could take the first letter of each concept: O, C, R, H, M, and E, and rearrange them to form the word "CHROME." If you could then recall simply that the methods of science were "shiny and clean like chrome," you could come up fairly quickly with the six methods that these letters stand for.

This general method can be used with a wide variety of materials and subject areas. For example, one student used the following device to recall the 12 disciples of Christ: "52 JaPs on MAB ST." (5 J's: two Johns, two Jameses, one Judas; 2 P's: Peter and Paul; and Matthew, Andrew, Bartholomew, plus Simon and Timothy.)

If you are a music student you may have used the following device to memorize the lines of the treble clef, which are E, G, B, D, and F. The mnemonic device is Every Good Boy Does Fine.

Psychology students use the name "ROY G. BeV" to recall the color spectrum (Red, Orange, Yellow, Green, Blue, Violet).

A medical student made up the following sentence for the purpose of recalling that of the 12 pairs of cranial nerves, the first, second, and eighth are sensory, the third, fourth, sixth, eleventh, and twelfth are motor, and the fifth, seventh, ninth and tenth are both sensory and motor.

1st–Some
2nd–Say
3rd–My
4th–Mother's
5th–Best
6th–Matzoh
7th–Ball
8th–Soup
9th–Barely
10th–Betters
11th–Moldy
12th–Meal

Note that the words, read down, form a meaningful (though silly) sentence, while the first letter of each word indicates sensory, motor, or both.

Single-Word Associations Suppose there is a particular fact, term or idea that you are having trouble recalling. (Assume you have rehearsed it time after time but continue to forget it as soon as you turn to another subject.) Sometimes you can come up with a single association that will plant this fact firmly in your memory forever. For example, this writer had trouble in college remembering which electromagnetic (light) wave lengths corresponded to red light and which corresponded to blue light. (Red is at the long end of the visible spectrum, that is, is produced by the longer of the visible wave lengths, while blue is produced by the shorter wave lengths.) I had once ridden a horse named "Big Red," whom I remembered quite vividly; by recalling this horse's name each time I wanted to recall the relative lengths of red and blue light, I could easily recall which was which.

You will undoubtedly be able to think of particular facts which you have trouble remembering; the same technique should prove useful.

Sentences and Stories   There is no need to rely solely on single words or short phrases to recall facts. One can take a number of key words or words which sound like the key words and construct a sentence or a story around them. For example, I once worked with a seventh-grade geography class in which the students had difficulty remembering the various countries in Central America and their relative location. I developed the following story for them to use which, in effect, lists the countries from north to south: Me (Mexico) gotta (Guatemala) new British Hondo (British Honduras and Honduras) on sale at the door (El Salvador), but this nickel car rag (Nicaragua) only cost (Costa Rica) me a penny, Ma (Panama).[3]

When I was nine years old, our family phone number was ATwater 9-7828. My mother thought up the following mnemonic device to enable us to remember the number: Atwater nine, seven had a toothache. An even better sentence might have been: AT Nine (9), Steven (7) ate (8) and had a tooth (2) ache (8). Incidentally, this is the only noncurrent phone number I have ever remembered for more than a few weeks.

There are any number of other areas where one might use this technique (e.g., to recall a particular sequence of historical events).

Rhymes   When you were younger you were probably taught rhymes such as "Thirty days has September, April, June, and November; all the rest have thirty-one excepting February alone"; or, "In fourteen hundred and ninety-two, Columbus sailed the ocean blue"; or "i before e, except after c, and when it's an 'a,' as in neighbor and

3.   British Honduras was recently renamed "Belize." How could you modify the above story so as to correctly recall the new name of this country?

weigh." There are many instances in which one can put a sequence of words together (each of which stands for some fact to be remembered) in such a way that they will rhyme. Because of the rhyme, the first part of the sequence makes the second (and later) parts easier to recall.

Rhythm Another mnemonic technique is the association of the rhythmic pattern of a familiar song or poem with material one wishes to recall. For example, consider the following list of names of famous early psychologists: Freud, Wundt, Wertheimer, Watson, James, and Hall. This list could be associated, in the order given, with the rhythm of the song "Row, Row, Row Your Boat, Gently Down the Stream." The precise matching is:

Row,   Row,   Row Your Boat, Gently Down the Stream
Freud, Wundt, Wertheimer,   Watson, James, and Hall

Observe that the rhythm pattern can indicate, among other things, the number of syllables in each word to be remembered (e.g., "Row" and "Freud" are one syllable; "Row Your Boat" and "Wertheimer" are three syllables). Rhythm patterns can, of course, be combined with rhymes further to facilitate recall.

The list just given does not exhaust all possible types of mnemonic devices, but you should find these sufficient to handle virtually any type of material you encounter for which such devices are suitable. Can you think up a mnemonic device to enable you to remember the six types of mnemonic devices just described?

There are three important cautions that must be made concerning the use of mnemonic devices for study purposes:

First, they should only be used when developing and remembering the devices themselves is easier, less time-consuming, or more effective than studying the material directly (e.g., rehearsing). If it is more trouble to think up and/or to remember your memory devices than it is to memorize the material by other methods, then obviously the devices are a waste of time in that context. It would be foolish, for example, to spend six hours thinking up good devices for a chapter of material when six hours of direct studying with rehearsal would bring much better results. You should not try to use mnemonic devices too extensively until you have had time to practice these techniques and have become skilled at using them. If you have to spend more than a few minutes thinking up mnemonics for a set of material, it is probably not worth your time.

The second caution is that if trying to use (one or more) mnemonic devices confuses you (makes everything a jumble, etc.), do not use them (or do not use the ones that confuse you). Some recent research indicates that if you use such devices despite the fact that you find them confusing, your memory may be impaired rather than improved.[4]

The third caution is that mnemonic devices are most appropriate for memorizing specific facts that fit no logical structure or concepts which cannot be easily integrated with each other in a logical sequence. Such devices are not a substitute for understanding material which requires abstract or integrative reading.

Summary

Passive rereading is of little help in programming memory. The best methods include: reading and rereading for understanding; establishing an intent to remember; rehearsal or recitation; and mnemonic devices. Six types of mnemonic aids are: mental images, words or phrases composed of key letters, single word associations, stories, rhymes, and rhythm. Mnemonic devices are most appropriate when: it is easier to make up the devices than to use other methods; the student is skilled at and not confused by using them; and the material has no inherent logical structure.

EXERCISES

Note: The exercises for this chapter require you to apply not only the principles discussed in Chapter 7, but also those discussed in previous chapters as well. If you can complete these exercises successfully, it will mean that you have understood and retained most of the important material discussed through Chapter 7.

1. For the selection below, do the following exercises *in the order indicated:*

  a. Glance at the heading in the selection in order to formulate reading purposes, including plans for remembering relevant information. Do this now.

  b. Read the passage, *underlining* (and/or bracketing) the main

4. J. J. Persensky and R. J. Senter, "The Effects of Subjects' Conforming to Mnemonic Instructions," *Journal of Psychology* 74 (1970), 15–20.

points and writing your reformulations of the concepts in the margins. Use symbols to indicate various categories and subcategories. Before doing this, indicate your system for noting varying degrees of importance (at least two levels).

_____   designation for items of most importance

_____   designation for items of secondary importance

_____   designation for items of less importance (optional)

SCIENTIFIC ATTITUDES AND THE INDUSTRIAL REVOLUTION

Before the French Revolution broke out, another type of revolution was under way in Europe. The term Industrial Revolution is used to describe the drastic changes in technology which transformed many aspects of Western European society. European technology had never been at a complete standstill; [there had been] advances in farming, in sailing, and in printing. . . . But the spirit of scientific inquiry which followed the Renaissance encouraged people to question old ways and seek new ways of doing things.

The men of the Renaissance had studied Greek teachings about observing in order to learn, experimenting to know facts, and reasoning from the facts in order to know the truth. The new scientific spirit went farther. First of all, scientists welcomed new facts. And then the scientists refused to deal with ideas or questions, like the purpose of man's life, his moral responsibility to other people, and the nature of the life to come. Science was based on the study of nature and the laws of nature. The early scientists agreed that the right method was to take one problem at a time, observing, testing, and describing what was learned about that before going on to the next subject.

. . . Sometimes a new discovery upset some

people so that they denied a scientist the freedom to question existing ideas. Galileo (1564–1642) is a well-known example. He built telescopes which enabled him to learn more about the planets. Galileo found additional proof of the idea which the Polish astronomer Copernicus (1473–1543) had put forward—that the earth revolved in an orbit around the sun, and that the earth also rotated on its axis. This discovery was contrary to the earlier Christian belief that the earth was stationary and that the sun revolved around the earth. High church leaders feared that the common people would lose faith in Christian teachings. Galileo was brought before the church court and forced to state that his facts were not true and that the earth did not move. According to the legend, Galileo said under his breath, "Nevertheless the earth moves."

Various branches of science were established by 1750. Astronomy went forward in spite of the attempt to check Galileo. Physics, including the study of motion and the study of light, developed. New inventions aided experimentation; the barometer was invented in Italy, the air pump in Germany, the microscope in Holland. A number of improvements were made in lenses for spectacles and magnifying glasses and telescopes. The physicist Robert Boyle began the experiments about gases and air that led to the discovery of oxygen and the beginning of chemistry as a branch of science.

Physiology developed out of the study of the human body. In 1628 William Harvey published his discovery that the blood circulates through the human body, driven by the pump-like heart. . . .

The results of scientific research were not applied to industry and agriculture at once. But the new spirit—the feeling that ways of doing things could and should be improved—began to affect people's everyday lives.

E. E. Ewing, *Our Widening World* (Chicago: Rand McNally, 1968), pp. 475–76.

c. Make "working notes," outlining the main points of the selection. Do this now.

d. After *actively rereading* the selection, indicate: (1) cause and effect relationships and (2) implications (including applications). (You might want to review the relevant sections in Chapter 4 before completing this exercise).

e. *Rehearse* the main points in the selection (including information noted in answer to questions posed as reading purposes and the material you have underlined, written in the margins, and put in your notes) by saying them to yourself again and again, until you can recite *all* the main points in the selection without once looking back at the material. When you have done this, complete item f *without looking back.* Do not look at item f until you have completed the above instructions.

f. Answer the following questions *without looking back* at the reading selection:

—What was the Industrial Revolution?

—How did scientific attitudes affect the Industrial Revolution?

—What were three major points in the new scientific attitudes?

—Name four branches of science established by the mid-eighteenth century.

2. Form mental images (mnemonic devices) to help you recall each of the following, making sure each image represents the *crucial aspects* of the thing to be remembered. Describe (or draw) the image(s) you formed in each case:

a. A girl named Sigafoos Klinghopper.

b. The English translation of the word *beurre* (pronounced "burr"), which is French for "butter."

c. The fact that Thomas Edison made the use of the electric light commercially feasible (or: Edison was basically responsible for the development of the electric industry in the U.S.).

3. Make up a word or words composed of letters (not necessarily only the first letters) in the names of Presidents VanBuren, Harrison, Tyler, Polk, and Taylor, in such a way that you will be able to recall them *in the proper order* (as given above). You might make up one word using letters from each of the names. If you use a nonsense word, be sure it is one you can recall easily. Or, you might make a list of five words each beginning with the same letter as one of the names. Since order is relevant here, the first word in the list would begin with "V," the second with "H," etc. The words should form a phrase (or sentence), to insure remembering the correct order and

the complete list. The words themselves need not relate to the names.

4. Invent a story that will connect all of the facts in the set below. You probably will never have to memorize such a list, but in order to practice using a story device, pretend that you do. Be sure the story *unifies* the facts or ideas to insure remembering the complete set of items. Also, make the story more than a mere paraphrased list of the facts or ideas to be remembered. (Note: You can use words that in some way *resemble* the key words to be learned.) Be sure your story enables you to associate corresponding events and dates.

Year	Event in U.S. History
1800	Federal government moves to Washington, D.C.
1801	John Marshall approved as Chief Justice of Supreme Court
1802	West Point Military Academy established
1803	Purchase of Louisiana Territory from France
1804	Vice President Burr kills Alexander Hamilton in a duel

5. Use *any device(s) you want* (image, word, phrase, or sentence composed of key letters; single-word association; story; rhythmic pattern; or rhyme) to remember each of the following (Note: You need not use one of the devices listed above if you can come up with a better one):

a. Your (or some friend's) telephone number (home, office, school, etc.), or a car license number, or an address. Describe your device.

b. The following list of groceries (avoid making another long list of words with no logical connection which will be no easier to memorize than the original): lemons, coffee, milk, dog food, lettuce, cokes, butter, frozen vegetables, macaroni, ice cream, potato chips, bread. Describe your device.

Evaluating Your Answers

1. Examples of acceptable answers:
   a. A useful set of reading purposes would be:

   What was the Industrial Revolution?
   How are scientific attitudes related to the Industrial Revolution?
   What are the "scientific attitudes" referred to (in the heading)?

b. A useful way of underlining the passage is shown below. Relevant classifications and summaries of some of the main ideas are shown in the margins. (Refer back to Chapter 5 for further details if necessary. Again, the notes in the right-hand margin indicate why certain terms or phrases were underlined. These notes are *not* the type which you should be making. They are simply to explain the reasons for *our* underlinings).

New spirit of scientific inquiry → Science began to affect every day lives... Industrial Revolution: drastic changes in technology

SCIENTIFIC ATTITUDES AND THE INDUSTRIAL REVOLUTION — Heading

Before the French Revolution broke out, another type of revolution was under way in Europe. The term Industrial Revolution is used to describe the drastic changes in technology which transformed many aspects of Western European society. European technology had never been at a complete standstill; [there had been] advances in farming, in sailing, and in printing. . . . But the spirit of scientific inquiry which followed the Renaissance encouraged people to question old ways and seek new ways of doing things.

— Topic sentence
— New concept and definition
— Causal relationship

Scientific Attitudes ① Greek ideas ② new spirit after Renaissance

    The men of the Renaissance had studied Greek teachings about (observing in order to learn, experimenting to know facts,) and reasoning from the facts in order to know the truth.) The new scientific spirit went farther. First of all, scientists welcomed new facts. And then the scientists refused to deal with ideas or questions, like the purpose of man's life, his moral responsibility to other people, and the nature of the life to come. Science was based on the study of nature and the laws of nature. The early scientists agreed that the right method was to take one problem at a time, observing, testing, and describing what was learned about that before going on to the next subject.

— List
— New concept and definition
— List

    . . . Sometimes a new discovery upset some people so that they denied a scientist the freedom to question existing ideas. (Galileo) (1564–1642) is a well-known example. He built telescopes which enabled him to learn more about the planets. Galileo found additional proof of the idea which

— Discovery

the Polish astronomer Copernicus (1473–1543) had put forward—that the earth revolved in an orbit around the sun) and that the earth also rotated on its axis. This discovery was(contrary to the earlier Christian belief)that the earth was stationary and that the sun revolved around the earth. High church leaders feared that the common people would lose faith in Christian teachings. Galileo was brought before the church court and forced to state that his facts were not true and that the earth did not move. According to the legend, Galileo said under his breath, "Nevertheless the earth moves."

③Various branches of science were established by 1750ⓐAstronomy went forward in spite of the attempt to check Galileo.ⓑPhysics, (including the study of motion and the study of light)developed. New inventions aided experimentation; the barometer was invented in Italy, the air pump in Germany, the microscope in Holland. A number of improvements were made in lenses for spectacles and magnifying glasses and telescopes. The physicist Robert Boyle began the experiments about gases and air that led to the discovery of oxygen and the beginning of chemistryⓒ as a branch of science.

ⓓPhysiology developed out of the study of the human body. In 1628 William Harvey published his discovery that the blood circulates through the human body, driven by the pump-like heart. . . .

(The results of scientific research were not applied to industry and agriculture at once.) But the new spirit—the feeling that ways of doing things could and should be improved—began to affect people's everyday lives.

Margin labels: Topic Sentence / List / Causal relationship / Discoveries / Discovery / Causal relationship

Handwritten note: New science went on in spite of setbacks.

c. Here is an example of a good set of working notes:

I. Scientific attitudes and the Industrial Revolution.
 A. Industrial Revolution: drastic technological changes
 B. New scientific spirit: led to changes, e.g., technology

1. Used Greek ideas
2. New ideas: get facts; focus on laws of nature; take one problem at a time; avoid certain subjects
3. New branches of science (and new equipment): astronomy (in spite of attempt to stop Galileo), physics, chemistry (Boyle—oxygen), physiology (Harvey—circulation)

d. The following are examples of correct answers:

Cause and effect relationships
—Post-Renaissance scientific attitudes led to men's search for better ways of doing things, e.g., better scientific methods and better technology.
—Galileo's discoveries prompted certain church leaders to force him to state his facts were false.
—New inventions led to better scientific experimentation.
—Robert Boyle's experiments led to the discovery of oxygen and to the start of the science of chemistry.
—Scientists' studies of the human body led to the beginning of the science of physiology.
Implications (including applications)
—It is valuable to use the methods of science employed by post-Renaissance scientists.
—You cannot change the facts by forcing someone to deny them.

f. The following are acceptable answers:

—The Industrial Revolution, beginning after the Renaissance, was when a vast number of technological developments were made, changing the way people lived.
—The post-Renaissance spirit of scientific inquiry strengthened the desire of men to find new ways of doing things.
—Major points in the new scientific attitude were:
   a. Scientists searched for new facts.
   b. Certain subjects were avoided.
   c. Scientists identified laws of nature.
   d. A scientist studied one problem at a time.
—Four branches of science established by the mid-eighteenth century were:

    a. Astronomy
    b. Physics
    c. Physiology
    d. Chemistry

2. Below are examples of acceptable answers. Each image contains all of the crucial aspects to be remembered:

    a. A cigar in a high-heeled shoe clinging to a grasshopper
    b. A stick of butter in the cold (brr) refrigerator
    c. A man with a banner across his chest saying, "Edison," screwing a lightbulb into a dollar-shaped socket on a map of the U.S.

3. A good answer using a phrase composed of key letters would be something like the following:

    Victor Hates Tom and Pleases Taylor.

On the other hand, consider a device such as:

    V.H.T.P.T.

This would be a poor mnemonic device, because it is not a phrase but merely a list of letters. The list has no inherent meaning and thus is not really a mnemonic device at all.

4. An example of an acceptable story would be:

    At 8:00 Sam got to Washington, and passed one courtly marshal who directed him to the two pointed gates at the fort. There he bought three kisses from French Louisa and killed four hams for Burt.

This device connects the events so that all of them will be remembered, and maintains the proper order (and thus the proper dates). On the other hand, an unacceptable "story" would be:

    In 1800 the government moved to D.C. So the next year John Marshall was made Chief Justice of the Supreme Court. The West Point Military Academy was started and in 1803 the government bought Louisiana from France. One year later Burr killed Hamilton.

This merely lists the events. There is no aid to remembering order or the complete list because there is no story using easily remembered ideas that stand for those to be memorized, nor a sequence which makes it easy to remember the correct order. (Contrast this story with the first one where, for example, one would not accidentally reverse the order of the first two events because one can visualize the character *first* arriving in the district and the same character *then* passing the district marshal: "At 8:00 Sam got to Washington and passed one courtly marshal."

5. This is an open-ended question and the answers shown are meant only to suggest some of the many possibilities.

a. If one is remembering numbers, sometimes it helps to associate the first or last pair in a series (or both) with some person (age, day or year of birth, etc.). This is similar to a single-word association. This procedure leaves fewer numbers to learn by rote. The following are examples of this technique.

> 386–2356   38 is my mother's age;
>   56 is my year of birth.

(The 6 and 23 would have to be recalled by other means.) A rhyme might be used in combination with key letters:

> BD 4128   Big Date—rhymes with 8.

(The 412 would have to be remembered by other means.)

To remember an address, one could use a rhythmic pattern; use a well-known pattern and substitute the address for the words.

> 2904 Sunny View Road   To   *mar*ket,   to   *mar*ket,
>   (Two *thou*sand, nine *hun*dred)
>
>   to   *buy* a   fat   *hog*.
>   (four *Sun-* ny View *Road*.)

b. Here are two good devices which combine the story method and use of key letters. The first one, which also uses numerals, is a clever solution invented by one student.

> Frozen Dog Island saw (looked out on) 4 cliffs (4 items starting with C, including ice *cream* and potato *chips*), 2 lands (2 items starting with L), 2 mountains (2 M's), and 2 beaches (2 B's).

> L. C.'s (lemon, coffee) mother (milk) let us (lettuce) cook (Coke) but (butter) Mac's (macaroni) well-bred (bread) dog (dog food) begs at the table (vegetables) and is cute (ice cream) but chipped a pot (potato chips).

You might also have used images to recall this list, e.g., a lemon sitting in a cup of coffee, floating in a pail of milk, which is perched on a package of dog food, surrounded by lettuce, etc. . . .

8. The Physical Context of Study

There are certain conditions of your physical surroundings that can have a substantial impact on your ability to study effectively.

Distractions

Ideally, the location where you study should be free of distractions. Potential distractions are of several types:

Auditory Distractions These include conversations with people in the same room; talking, laughing, singing, and yelling by people in neighboring rooms; sounds emanating from radios, TVs, telephones, and record players; and street noise. Preferably, you should study in a location that is free from such distractions, e.g., a library, an isolated room, or a study center.

This does not necessarily mean that you should study in a place where there is absolutely no noise at all. This might also be distracting, since you are probably not used to total silence. A regular, low-intensity background noise such as that made by a fan or air-conditioning unit is ideal in that it provides some noise and yet is minimally distracting.

This type of noise also helps to mask or block out any other (irregular) background sounds that occur. Some students insist that they study most effectively with background music, because of its ability to mask other sounds. This writer advises against background music, however, because it is distracting in itself. If nevertheless you insist upon it, you can at least minimize its distracting qualities by playing the music on low volume, playing instrumental rather than vocal pieces, and choosing the type of music which you personally find least distracting.

You should also recognize that if you are constantly *aware* of the music when you study, it means that you are not fully concentrating on your studying. (One student claimed that this was precisely why he used it—as a method of monitoring his degree of concentration. As will be seen in a later chapter, however, there is a more direct method of monitoring your mental operations while studying.)

Experimental studies have found that the more intense the background noise, the greater the effort required to concentrate in its presence. Even though concentration *can* be maintained in the presence of loud noise if the individual is highly motivated, such concentration is attained at a higher cost in terms of fatigue than is the case with lower intensity noise.

Visual Distractions   These stem primarily from the area immediately surrounding the area in which you work, e.g., irrelevant "clutter" on the desk, wall posters, windows, food, etc. Keeping your work area free of all materials except those you need for studying will minimize such distractions. Many students claim that pictures of loved ones are especially distracting and should not be directly visible from their work area. If you study in a library, try to find a location that is relatively free of movement (especially irregular movement), so that you will not be tempted to look at each person who enters, leaves, or passes by.

Interruptions   There is another type of distraction which is both auditory and visual. It consists of other individuals continually coming up to you or calling you while you are studying and asking for help, advice, favors, attention, etc. Such interruptions often destroy the "mental set" you have established toward the material you are learning. Establishing this mental set requires bringing to mind the relevant prior knowledge and the current reading purposes needed to understand the material you are studying. Getting back "into the groove" after interruptions can be difficult, time-consuming, and fatiguing, especially if the material is complex.

It is not only the interruptions themselves which must be avoided but the *expectation* of interruption. If you are constantly expecting to be interrupted, it will be difficult to establish the proper mental set in the first place. Thus it is advisable to find a time and location where you can *anticipate* substantial periods of uninterrupted study.

One final point about distraction in general. One group of researchers found that when students attempt to remove distractions from their study environment, they initially find it distracting! This is because the removal of the sound or sight is a change from what they have become accustomed to. Thus they recommend that you try out any changes of this type for a minimum of *two weeks* before expecting any improvements in your study effectiveness.[1]

Are any of the above types of distractions a problem for you? If so, what can you do to correct the situation?

Regular Study Location and Time

Almost all study-skills experts recommend that you establish a regular study location or locations, e.g., specific buildings, rooms, chairs, desks, etc. The function of this procedure is to associate these locations in your mind with studying. The assumption is that this puts you in less conflict than you would be in if you studied, for example, in bed where you also sleep, or on the lawn where you can also sunbathe.

Some students object to this suggestion, however, on the grounds that it is unnecessary. More important than regularity of location, they argue, is the attitude the student has toward studying. A well-motivated student, they assert, can study in many different locations.

One cannot dispute this argument except to note that all students are *not* highly motivated, and therefore need to do everything they can to encourage and facilitate studying. Establishing a regular study location, therefore, can be of substantial help. Furthermore, as implied above, some study locations involve far more distractions than others.

Many students find that instead of or in addition to a fixed location, *studying at the same time(s) each day* facilitates the development of good habits. This time may be early in the morning, between class periods, after lunch, after dinner, late at night, or some combination

1. W. W. Farquhar, J. D. Krumboltz, and C. G. Wrenn, *Learning to Study* (New York: Ronald, 1960), pp. 57–58.

of these. You may want to experiment with the idea of regular study times as a supplement to or as an alternative to the idea of a regular study location.

Organization

To minimize wasted time and effort it is helpful to organize your study area so that all the materials which you will need (e.g., pencils, pens, felt-tip markers, paper, textbooks, dictionary, etc.) are collected before you begin studying. This will save unnecessary trips and will make it harder to rationalize not studying!

Physical Comfort

Physical discomfort is by its nature distracting as well as fatiguing. Thus, if possible, try to find a study location where the temperature, ventilation, and humidity are to your liking. An overly warm work location is especially to be avoided, because it will tend to make you drowsy.

A comfortable place to sit is also important. Study-skills experts recommend an upright posture in a chair that is comfortable but not too comfortable, so that you will not fall asleep. Many students insist, however, that their bed is the only really comfortable place in their room and claim that they can study perfectly well on it without falling asleep. If you can do it, fine; but if you frequently find yourself falling asleep, trying sitting someplace that is slightly less comfortable and where you can easily maintain an upright posture.

Lighting

There are only two basic principles here: have enough light to study without strain, and use a method of lighting that avoids glare. Glare occurs when: there is too much contrast between the amount of light in your study area and the light in the rest of the room; or between the material being read and its immediate background; or where the light source is too sharply focused rather than diffused; or when the light shines directly into your eyes rather than being placed well behind and/or above your work location.

Surroundings Do Not Make You Study

It is important to recognize that a good physical study environment will not, by itself, force you or "condition" you to study or to learn. Studying is accomplished with your mind, not with pencils, lights, chairs, and music. The physical environment can make your studying easier or harder, but it will not initiate and sustain the mental effort that learning requires. This must be done by you.

Summary

The physical environment most conducive to effective study is free of major auditory and visual distractions and of interruptions; involves regularity of location and/or time; is well organized; is comfortable; and has adequate lighting with a minimum of glare.

9. The Social Context of Study

Many students like to engage in what is called "group studying," that is, studying with the active participation of one or more other persons. Studying with other individuals can be of help in some circumstances, but there are also many pitfalls which you should be aware of. Let us first consider the conditions under which studying with others can be helpful.

Benefits of Group Study

To Aid Understanding   Sometimes, even after conscientiously studying some idea or passage, you may find that its meaning is still not clear to you. In such a case you may find it helpful to go to a friend (or teaching assistant, or instructor, or professor) for an explanation. If you go to a friend, it will probably be someone who is enrolled in the course or who has taken the course or its equivalent before.

If you have difficulty with the course as a whole, you may want to find a regular *tutor*. Often the study skills or counseling center at your college will help you to find a suitable person.

Incidentally, acting as a tutor yourelf will often increase *your* un- **95** derstanding of the material, because it forces you to conceptualize, in your own words, the basic ideas you are trying to explain (see Chapter 3).

To Test Understanding and Recall   Just as other persons can help explain a concept to you, they can also test your understanding and your recall of the material you studied. Thus before an exam you could sit down with one or two other students and ask each other questions about the assigned material. Students who have difficulty being objective about judging the extent of their own understanding and recall may find this process helpful. (However, for reasons to be discussed later, it is a poor idea to depend habitually upon others to do your self-testing for you.)

Another reason for having another person test you before an exam is to practice "performing under pressure." Such practice will help reinforce the connections in your mind and give you added confidence in your ability to answer such question in an exam setting.

To Facilitate Integrations   If the subject you are preparing is very complex, or if it is to be tested by an essay exam, you may find that discussing the material with others will suggest integrations (e.g., themes, similarities, differences, etc.) that would not have occurred to you on your own. In the process of working out answers to questions brought up by others or working through connections suggested by them you may gain a deeper understanding of the material yourself.

Pitfalls of Group Study

Despite the helpful aspects of studying with others, there are a number of possible drawbacks to group study.

Pseudo-Studying in Groups   There is a phenomenon called "pseudo-studying" which sometimes occurs in group sessions. It goes something like this: A student who has not studied the material thoroughly gets together with other students to test understanding and recall in preparation for an exam. Each person asks a question and some other person tries to answer it. After all the material has been covered, it is observed that every question that was asked was answered by somebody in the group. The student who has not studied the material, and who himself answered few if any of the questions, then concludes: "We know this material cold." Subconsciously he substitutes "I" for "we" and convinces himself that *he personally* knows the material. Then he takes his exam, gets most of the answers wrong, and is astonished that he did so poorly in view of all the "studying" he did. The student has deceived himself into thinking that he knows what the members of the group as a whole know, forgetting that on a test the questions are answered by individuals, not groups.

Group Dependency The student who studies with other people can easily become dependent on them to do his thinking for him. Pseudo-group study is one manifestation of such dependency. Other expressions of group dependency in study are: seeking the help of others whenever you cannot understand some concept or idea on your own immediately, without any effort; always having others test your understanding because you have made no effort to learn to evaluate your own knowledge objectively; and taking others' opinions about some idea as true simply because they act confident, even though they give no reasons for their opinion, etc.

It cannot be emphasized too strongly that studying and learning (that is, understanding, remembering, etc.) are activities of individuals, not of groups. Others can help you to understand and help test your understanding, but they cannot do the actual mental work for you. Understanding is an individual process. You do not automatically know something just because someone in your study group knows it or tells you about it. At best, group study is a supplement to, not a substitute for, individual study.

One way to insure that you do not become overly dependent on others is to always study alone both before and after you study in a group. Do as much as you can on your own, and make sure that you personally understand the ideas discussed in the group sessions.

Bull and Gossip Sessions It is very easy, especially when the group members are close personal friends, for the topic of conversation to stray from the material to be studied into discussions about other unrelated topics. This can even happen when the members are not close friends—when, for example, one member associates something in the assigned material with some personal experience or insight having no direct relevance to the course, and others follow suit.

In order to minimize wasted time and effort, it is important that group study sessions be consistently *task-centered*. When the discussion wanders from the main point, someone should see to it that attention is refocused on the original purpose of the session.

Overly Large Groups The student will usually find that the time spent in group studying will be used efficiently in direct proportion to the smallness of the group. The larger the group, the more likely you are to encounter irrelevant comments, delays, interruptions, excessive noise, differences in ability that make some people bored and others confused, mixed purposes and motives for attending, and the like. If you are going to engage in group study you may find that a group of two (you and one other person) will prove to be the optimum size. You should, of course, choose the other person carefully so that both of you derive some benefit from the sessions.

Time Waste   Even under the best of conditions (small groups, task-centered discussions, thorough advance preparations) you will find that group study is more time-consuming than individual study. Thus, if you are habitually pressed for time, you may find that group sessions are not worth the benefits obtained. Some students suggest putting a firm *time limit* on all group study sessions, so that they do not drag on endlessly.

Do any of the above pitfalls of group study apply to you? If so, what can you do to correct the problem?

Summary

Group studying can be beneficial as an aid to understanding; as a method of testing understanding and recall; and as a means of facilitating integrations. However, certain pitfalls of group studying should be carefully avoided: pseudo-studying, in which the student subconsciously seduces himself into believing that he knows what the other group members know; group dependency; study sessions that degenerate into bull and gossip sessions; overly large groups which cannot be coordinated efficiently; and the spending of time that might be better used in individual study.

10. How To Manage Time

College students sometimes get into academic trouble simply because they fail to utilize their time efficiently. These problems are of two opposite types: time underutilization and time overload.

Time Underutilization

Underutilization involves waste; it means failing to make the most of what you have. Time wastage is usually traceable to a lack of *purposefulness*. To lack purpose means not to know what you are after or how to get it. Among students the cause of this state is typically a lack of adequate motivation for college. (If this is your problem, you may want to skip ahead to Part II.) Psychologically, purposelessness is often associated with immaturity. A hallmark of immaturity is an inability to hold a long-range time perspective; an immature person feels that the future is not real and therefore is unable to plan for it.

Some students have long-range goals (or at least short-range goals) but fail to focus fully on how their everyday actions relate to these goals. Time slides by, so to speak, unnoticed—just as if they had no goals. **99**

Examine the following types of wasted time and ask yourself if any of them apply to you.

—The "warming-up" or "getting ready to study" routine that goes something like this: Sam Student sits down at his desk to study but then decides he must first sharpen his pencil. Returning to his desk he decides that the light needs to be adjusted. Next he finds that the radio (which is probably too loud anyway) needs tuning. Just then he hears a noise and decides to tell the guy in the hall to keep quiet. Arriving back at his desk he notices his checkbook and wonders if he has enough in the bank to buy that new shirt he saw the day before. Suddenly he remembers that he failed to make an "important" phone call; on the way back, he checks with a friend about the date of an upcoming exam. Then, feeling somewhat tired, he decides to get a cup of coffee. Noticing a friend in the lounge, he chats for a few minutes and then decides to catch the end of the TV program. When he returns to his room, he has to look for his textbook and the syllabus. He finds his chair is uncomfortable so he moves to the bed. Then, exhausted from a long evening of "study," he falls asleep, vowing to get up and do his work early the next morning. However, when the alarm goes off, he just can't seem to get up, and so on . . .

—Procrastinating about getting up in the morning, even when you can no longer sleep and have things to do.

—Wandering around campus between classes when you could be reading or doing homework.

—Extending meals for an extra hour after you are finished, even when talking to the people at the table does not really interest you and interferes with other goals.

—Unnecessary travel to and from school, the dorm, or the library due to the failure to plan trips in advance or to choose the most convenient study location.

—"Bull sessions" engaged in not because you find them interesting, relaxing, or informative, but just to "do something."

—Watching TV or playing cards even when you know you do it too much.

—Excessive group studying.

—Extensive fantasy, elaborate daydreams, fiddling, fidgeting, and endless rationalization during all of these time-wasting activities.

There is no implication intended that discussions, watching TV, card-playing, coffee drinking, or making phone calls are in any way wrong or irrational in themselves. They only become so when they are engaged in not for their own sake or for the sake of some future goal, but as rationalizations for avoiding work that one thinks one should do and yet does not want to do.

Virtually all study-skills experts recommend making a study schedule as a means of increasing your awareness of the importance of time management and as an aid to allocating time.

How To Make a Study Schedule The most detailed type of study schedule involves blocking out each day on an hour-by-hour basis. Regular activities such as eating, traveling, and classes are then entered in the appropriate blocks. The remaining blocks are filled in with specific assignments to be completed or subjects to be studied during each hour period (e.g., "study French"; "Psychology, read ch. 8"; "start English book"; etc.). Leisure-time activities and rest periods can also be entered on the schedule. Each day or week is blocked out in advance in this fashion.

The length of time devoted to each subject is proportional to the difficulty of the material, the specific demands of the course (e.g., upcoming exams require extra time), and the length of time you can make yourself concentrate at one sitting.

The schedule is usually written on a printed appointment book, a notebook, a ruled sheet of paper, or even a small blackboard.

The motivational assumption of the study-skills experts is that having a written schedule will provide an incentive to get the assigned task completed, and that completing it will yield a sense of satisfaction and heighten the desire to attain future study goals.

Talking with students who have contemplated or tried using study schedules, however, indicates that such schedules are far from a panacea for poor time management and that they may even have certain disadvantages.

Objections to Making a Study Schedule One objection to telling a student to make a schedule, divorced from the wider context of his study motivation in general, is that nothing compels him to *keep* to his schedule. Students who have little motivation to study in the first place are not usually helped by the act of *making* a schedule. When they do make one, they typically ignore it.

A more universal complaint about making a detailed schedule is that it is too rigid and inflexible. Students argue that they cannot always anticipate how long an assignment will take, or when an exam date will be announced, or when some unexpected event will force them to change their plans. Having to break their intended schedule may cause them conflict and guilt, which may undermine existing study motivation.

Detailed schedules also fail to anticipate the student's mood; for example, the schedule may say to study French when one is in the mood to study English. If one sticks to the schedule anyway, study motivation may be undermined. On the other hand, if one changes it whenever the mood strikes, what good is the schedule?

In view of these arguments, it does not seem possible to make any universal generalizations about whether or not a detailed study schedule will be helpful to an individual student. Some students find schedules to have no effect on them one way or the other; others swear by them; and still others claim schedules do more harm than good. You will have to decide for yourself on this matter after considering the pros and cons.

Alternatives to a Detailed Study Schedule   It should be mentioned that there are other possibilities besides no study schedule or a detailed, written schedule. Some students find that simply making a written *list* of things to be accomplished during the day or week is adequate. A very general schedule indicating the subjects to be worked on each day is sufficient for others. Still other students are able to hold their goals in their head and stick to them.

Whichever method you choose, remember that sufficient use of your time requires *some* form of future planning, including implicit or explicit goal-setting. The basic principle to follow is that *each day you spend in college should have a purpose or purposes.* These daily purposes should in turn be related to your longer-range goals.

Reward Yourself for Reaching Goals   Whether you make a detailed study schedule or simply a list of study purposes for the week, you should also make specific plans to reward yourself for attaining your daily or weekly goals. These rewards should involve activities which you enjoy for their own sake, e.g., pleasure reading; dating; listening to radio, TV, or records; informal chit-chat with a friend; going out for a snack; playing cards; etc. It is usually preferable to postpone these daily or weekly rewards until *after* you have attained your goals; this will give you something to look forward to while studying and will enable you to enjoy your leisure activities without guilt or anxiety. (Be careful, however, not to rush through your work by doing perceptual-level reading just to get done!)

Time Overload

This problem involves trying to do too much with your time. There are three major sources of time overload among college students.

Excessive Study Load   Students who flunk or drop courses often attempt to "make up" all these courses by taking an extra-heavy load in subsequent semesters. Unfortunately, they frequently end up doing just as poorly or more poorly than before, because in addition to the problems that caused them trouble previously (such as poor motivation or study habits), they now have more work than they can handle. If you cannot maintain a load of, say, four courses a semester, do not try to make up for it by taking 5 or 6 courses the next semester until and unless you *know* that you can and will handle such a load.

One reason students overload themselves is because they base their load on their wishes, hopes, or fears rather than on relevant facts, such as their actual demonstrated capacity and motivation. Students may also overload themselves not because they want to but because somebody else wants them to or because they are comparing themselves to somebody else. One student admitted to me that he overloaded himself because of peer group pressure and a feeling of inferiority to others who had higher loads.

Another student once told me that he was in conflict because his current course load (which in this case was the normal load) in a difficult graduate curriculum was more than he could handle. He had a great deal of trouble with some of the required courses, and he had his own standards of what he considered to be good scholarship, which he did not feel he could meet under his present load. But the dean, while not forbidding a course reduction, had made him feel guilty about wanting to reduce it, and had also indicated that something was "wrong" with him because other students were not reducing their loads.

I told him that he was the best judge of what he could handle and what he could not, and that if the dean did not personally like it, that was the dean's problem, not his. Furthermore, I told him that the real issue was between *him and reality* (that is, between him and the courses) *not between him and society's* (e.g., the dean's) *interpretation of reality*. Different students have different standards and different capacities, and these factors should be their guide in choosing a course load (within the limits of what is allowed by the rules), not what other people are doing. In short, I told him to use his own judgment in the matter, not the arbitrary assertions or the actions of some third party who knew little or nothing about his particular abilities and values.

Some students, however, are not to blame for their overly heavy loads, which are due to scholarship or curriculum requirements that cannot be avoided. In such cases the student's only alternatives are: to select his courses so that he does not have too many difficult, time-consuming ones at the same time; and to avoid, as much as possible, the other types of overload to be described below.

Part Time Jobs   Many students are compelled for financial reasons to take part-time jobs to pay for all or part of their college expenses. In addition to the time such jobs take away from study, they may leave the student too tired to study for extended periods when he is through work.

Again the resolution of this problem may be difficult. Some possibilities are: reducing one's course load; taking jobs that are closer to home or campus or that are less tiring; working fewer hours per week; or finding alternative means of financial support (student loans, etc.).

Leisure and Recreation   Leisure and recreation are appropriate and desirable activities for students to engage in. Sometimes, however, these activities are so time-consuming that they seriously interfere with study. Most commonly they involve romantic relationships; sports; hobbies; and work in student organizations or clubs.

If the student discovers that he is trying to engage in too many outside activities, he will have to make a decision as to which of his goals are most important to him and then drop those activities which are not furthering or which are inhibiting the attainment of those goals.

Pseudo-overload

In all cases of apparent time overload, before making decisions as to changing course load or jobs or extracurricular activities, the student should check to make sure that he is efficiently utilizing the time he does have. There is a phenomenon called "pseudo-overload" which appears to involve overload but actually involves underutilization. The symptoms are the feeling of being in constant motion and "never having time" to do anything and yet never seeming to get anything done. Sometimes this is called "spinning one's wheels." It appears as though there is a shortage of time, whereas in fact available time is "frittered away" on trivial activities, or by procrastination, or by constantly starting tasks that are never finished, or by indecisiveness in deciding on one's course of action. The solution in this case is not to find more time but to use the time one has more efficiently.

What about you? Do you have a time underutilization problem? A time overload problem? Or is it pseudo-overload? What can you do to resolve these problems?

Summary

The two main ways that students mismanage time are by wasting it and by trying to do too much. Wasted time is often due to lack of purpose, which results in numerous types of unproductive activities (daydreaming, etc.). One way to encourage better use of time is to make a detailed study schedule, although some students find this too rigid and prefer lists of goals for the day or week. The student should reward himself for attaining study goals by engaging in valued leisure activities after goal attainment. Time overload is typically due to: too heavy a course load; time-consuming and/or fatiguing outside jobs; and excessive extra-curricular activities such as dating, sports, club work and hobbies. Pseudo-overload refers to the appearance of overload caused by time being spent on unproductive activities.

11. How To Take Lecture Notes

As implied in Chapter 1, class or lecture notes play a far more important role in college than in high school. In some courses *completely new material* is presented in the lectures, that is, material which is not available in the readings or anywhere else. Often this material represents the lecturer's own (unpublished) views on the subject being discussed. In other courses, the lectures *expand* and *elaborate* on the readings and help to *organize* them in a way that the instructor considers meaningful. Some teachers use the lectures mainly to *clarify and explain* the reading, especially where the subject matter is complex. Others use lectures as a means of indicating to the student what is *important* in the course. Some classes are simply question and answer sessions combined with class discussion. And there are even a few teachers who use class periods to rehash, word for word, exactly what is in the text. In most courses, the lectures will play, in varying degrees, several of these roles.

Except where lectures repeat exactly what is in the text or where class discussions are meaningless, it is imperative that the student attend lectures regularly, since exams are likely to be based, at least in part, on this material. To get a precise idea of what role the lectures play, *you are advised to ask the teacher directly at the beginning of the course*!

Reading versus Lecture Note-taking

Two important differences between lecture note-taking and the taking of reading notes have action implications for the student.

Need for Alertness   If you read a passage in a book and fail to understand it because you were not in full focus, you can always reread the passage. If you miss part of a lecture, however, *it is gone forever.* Unless you ask the professor to repeat (which you will probably not want to do too often), there is no way to get what you missed except by asking another student. What you get from him may be uninterpretable, or incomplete, or it may be written from a very subjective point of view. There is no substitute for getting your notes first-hand. This requires that you listen carefully to everything that is said.

Need for Completeness   Notes taken on reading are usually only a summary of the main points. This is adequate since you can always go back to the book for details. Lecture material, however, is like a book being read to you. Since your notes are your *only* source, they must be complete if they are to be useful. This does not mean that you should take down every word the lecturer says, but you should definitely take down more than just the highlights (see below for details).

Common Errors in Lecture Note-taking

Errors of Omission   Study-skills textbooks typically warn the student not to take "too many" notes and not to take "too few" notes. After an extensive study of the lecture notes of 181 students from 12 different courses at the University of Maryland, I have concluded that the first type of error is extremely rare among students. When students' lecture notes were compared on an idea-by-idea basis with what the 12 course instructors considered to be good notes (defined as notes which would be taken by an "A" student), it was found, on the average, that *fewer than 60 percent of these ideas or facts were recorded by students in their notes.* If this average is subdivided according to facts or ideas that were written on the blackboard versus those that were not, over 88 percent of the former and less than 52 percent of the latter were found to be in students' notes. This means that, excluding what the professor puts on the blackboard, *the average student is omitting from his notes close to half of the material the professor believes to be important.*

What are the causes of these omissions?

Misconceptions as to the need for good lecture notes.   As already noted, some students do not realize how important lecture notes are in college courses in general, nor do they identify the specific role played by such notes in their particular courses. By finding out this information as soon as possible after the course begins and by being aware that lecture notes are generally more important in college than in high school, you can avoid these errors.

As a practical recommendation, especially in view of the findings just reported, you would do well to take *more* extensive notes than you think are needed. If you actually do take too many you can always condense them later, whereas if you take too few you cannot easily retrieve the missing material.

Fatigue and boredom.   The note-taking study found what appeared to be a fatigue or boredom effect in lecture note-taking. There was a 15 percent average increase in errors of omission in the second 30 minutes of the 12 lectures studied. Lectures that were longer than 60 minutes showed another 15 percent increase in omissions over the second 30 minutes. The best way to avoid this error is to anticipate it by increasing one's efforts of concentration during the latter part of each lecture. (See also Chapter 15.)

Boredom induced by the content of the lecture or by the style of delivery may also cause lapses of attention. These are best handled by reminding yourself of the importance of the lectures to the course, the importance of the course in attaining your degree, and the importance of your degree in furthering your career goals. If the lectures are totally intolerable, try dropping the course and switching to another.

(Over-)Integrating during the lecture.   It was noted in Chapter 4 that integrations play a crucial role in understanding reading material. The same goes for lecture material. However, for the most part integrations of the lecture material should take place *after* rather than during the lecture. The reason is that integrating takes time, and during most lectures there is usually only time for note-taking as such. If you begin making complex integrations, you may miss important points which the lecturer is discussing or you may fail to understand clearly what he is saying. If associations do occur to you during the lecture, make a brief notation in one of the margins of your notebook and come back to the idea later.

Excessive speed of lecture.   Some lecturers go so fast that it is hard to keep up with them. The best solution, if you find yourself halfway through one point while the lecturer is already halfway through the next point, is to ask him politely to slow down. He has no way of knowing that he is going too fast unless you tell him.

Some teachers tend to speed up at the end of a lecture in order to cover all the material they intended to cover. If interruptions late in the lecture are not feasible, ask the teacher to review this material at the beginning of the next lecture.

Another way to cope with a fast lecturer is to use a "personal shorthand" consisting of abbreviations which are meaningful to you and which can be retranslated by you later as necessary. You will have to tailor-make some abbreviations (e.g., of frequently used technical terms) on a course-by-course basis. Abbreviations for commonly used words (like "and," "with," "but," and "therefore") can be used in a variety of different courses.

Trying to get every word. The overwhelming majority of students are likely to take too few rather than too many notes. Paradoxically, however, one cause of taking too few notes is *trying* to take too many. If you try to take down everything the lecturer says, word for word, you are likely to become so confused and get so far behind that your notes will be totally inadequate. Lecture note-taking, like reading, must be selective. Taking thorough and complete lecture notes does not mean writing down everything the teacher says but rather everything that you judge to be important. You can think of proper lecture note-taking as the equivalent of proper underlining; take down everything that you would underline in a textbook. Or, to be on the safe side, take down a little more than this.

Difficulty in understanding. Occasionally you may find that there comes a point in a given lecture where you get lost. This may be because the material itself is very complex, or because the lecturer is confusing, or because you had not been listening during the previous ten minutes, or because you had not done the recommended reading in preparation for the lecture. (If advance reading is recommended by the instructor, you will do well to take his advice).

There are several possibilities open to you if you get lost: ask the teacher to explain the material again; get help from a friend after class; go to the teacher or teaching assistant during office hours; get a tutor; or drop the course. The latter solution is recommended if you are lost during most of every lecture.

Be careful of the tendency to react emotionally when you are temporarily confused and simply "give up" for the remainder of the lecture. You will often find that what at first seems confusing will become clear if you keep trying to understand it; furthermore, the confusing part of the lecture may be followed by material that is more easily understood, providing you remain in focus.

Distractions. In order to avoid being distracted during lectures, try not to sit near open windows, entrances into and exits from the lecture hall, or overly talkative friends. If you sit next to a girl-friend or boy-friend, make a mutual agreement that during the lecture you will pay attention mainly to the lecture rather than to each other.

Difficulty in seeing and hearing.   If there are problems, sit closer to the front. Most students do not like to be too visible to the lecturer, so there are usually plenty of seats in the first few rows. Furthermore, by sitting near the front of the class you are more likely to attain eye contact with the teacher and even get to know him. As a result you are more likely to become "involved" in the course and hence to pay attention to and understand what is being said.

Errors of Commission   Errors of omission in lecture notes are by far the most common variety. But occasionally there will be errors of commission. Errors of commission occur when the student records some definition, idea, fact, or explanation given by the lecturer but does it incorrectly (e.g., "1796" for "1769," "was" for "was not," etc.)

Sometimes this is due to a misunderstanding of what the lecturer said, caused by failure to pay sufficient attention on your part, or by poor enunciation or inadequate speech volume on his part. One way to catch such errors is to see whether what the teacher says at one time contradicts what he says at another time. If this occurs, it is possible that you misunderstood him at least one of the times. You can also check with a friend or with the teacher himself.

Errors of commission can also be due to subjectivism (see Chapter 3). It is a mistake, for example, to take down what the lecturer says in your own words rather than in the words he uses, since you run the risk of distorting his intended meaning. While reformulating ideas in your own words is an important aid to understanding (Chapter 3), it should be done (when needed) *after* rather than during the lecture. During the lecture there is not sufficient time to translate what is said and to insure its accuracy. Also the professor may want you to use the wording he gives you, especially if he is defining some new, technical term or identifying some important rule, law, or principle. The main clue here is that if the teacher wants you to know his exact wording, he will give the definition slowly and will probably repeat it at least once.

Taking lecture notes is primarily a matter of *selective recording*, not one of interpretation or integration. These operations come later, when you study the notes.

Inadequate Note Paper and/or Margins   I once had a student who took lecture notes in a notebook measuring 2½-by-3½ inches. Among other things, this makes for a great many notebooks by the time the course is over. Also it makes integrating and organizing difficult, because one cannot see enough of the material at one time to grasp how it fits together. Regular 8½-by-11-inch ruled paper is recommended. Keeping the notes in a three-ring binder allows you to avoid carrying around (and possibly losing) all of your notes for a given course.

Leaving 1- to 3-inch margins to the left and/or right of your actual notes provides space for reformulations, integrations (with readings, etc.) and other relevant comments. You can use these margins just like you use the margins of your textbook (see Chapter 5).

To illustrate some of the differences between good and poor lecture notes, samples of two students' notes from one course are shown in Table 1. One set of notes was made by a student who received a grade of A in the course, the other by a student who received an F.

The most striking difference between the notes of the A student and the F student is the greater detail in the notes of the former. In fact the A student's notes contain close to 60 percent more material than those of the F student. Note that the poorer student seems to simply give up in the middle of some sentences. In addition, this student makes some serious errors of commission, e.g., "Fraud" instead of "Freud," "preserving" instead of "perceiving."

While the A student's notes for this part of this lecture were basically good, they were by no means perfect. The material in brackets indicates some of the material which the A student omitted. Note, however, that most of the omitted material is not too essential and some of it might have been added if the student had edited his notes after class.

Using Your Lecture Notes

It is recommended that you go over your lecture notes for each lecture *as soon as possible after the lecture.* There are a number of reasons why this procedure is beneficial.

Editing   One reason for rereading notes is editing. This involves, for example, filling in obvious omissions, correcting "typographical" errors, expanding personal abbreviations (if necessary), and tidying up illegible handwriting. If you don't do these things soon after the lecture, you are likely to forget so much that you will be unable to do them later.

Table 1. Comparison of Lecture Notes of A and F Students (Part of One Lecture in Introductory Psychology Class)

F Student's Notes	A Student's Notes
What is Psychology? definitions:	Psychology: What is it?
1. Psychology is the study of the contain of the conscious mind.	1. Original view, Wundt, [the] 1st psychologist: study of the structural-[structure and]-content of the conscious mind, immediate conscious experience.
2. Fraud; Psychoanalysis is the second view of psychology, basically the study of the unconscious	2. Freud, [founder of] Psychoanalysis: study of the unconscious.
3. Watson; Behaviorism—should not study the mind but only the things you can observe, smiling, crying, etc.	3. Watson, [founder of] Behaviorism: observable behavior—rejecting [the concept of] consciousness or [and] unconsciousness. Introspection not considered. Environmental stimuli [studied instead]. Ignores concept of identity—ignores causality*. . .
Psychology studies the attributes and characteristics	[4. Preferred definition] Psychology is the science that studies the attributes and characteristics which certain conscious living organisms possess; [by virtue of being conscious. This definition includes the study of the] contents of consciousness, [observable] behaviors, content of [sub-] unconscious mind.
What is The faculty for preserving reality	Consciousness
1. The first function of consciousness is cognition	1. The faculty for perceiving reality by the use of senses and reason=*cognition*.
2. Motivation	2. Faculty for appraising and evaluating reality; [studies] emotions, needs=*motivation*.
Basic Methods of Psychology Introspection: A systematic observation	Basic Methods of Psychology All [those] already mentioned [as methods] of science* plus introspection [which is] unique to psychology. [Introspection is] systematic observation turned inwards; [it is an act of conceptual identification directed] towards [one's own] mental contents and processes . . . *Discussed in an earlier part of this lecture.

Underlining   Although lecture notes are themselves selective, you can still underline them as you would a text in order to indicate various degrees of importance (see Chapter 5). What is most important will be recalled most clearly right after the lecture.

Organizing   It is crucial to insure that your lecture notes have a clear organization. It is especially important that they have clearly designated major and minor headings to indicate the categories and subcategories into which the lecture material falls. A good lecturer will help you to do this by, for instance, writing a lecture outline on the blackboard. But if he does not do it, you must do it yourself. (If you have to organize or reorganize the material yourself, do it after the lecture, since you will probably not have time to do it carefully during the lecture. Furthermore, imposing a premature organization on the material may lead to confusion.) Clear organization of your material is essential if you are to avoid the total chaos that would result from a lengthy jumble of unrelated facts and statements (see Chapter 4).

Reformulating and Integrating   If you can think of relevant integrations between different parts of the lecture, or between one lecture and another, or between lectures and reading, you can write these observations in the margin(s) of your notes after you have had time to think about them (see Chapter 4). At the same time you can reformulate any of the ideas or concepts that were difficult to understand (see Chapter 3). Again this is best done when the material is fresh in your mind. (Additional integrating can be done, however, when you are studying for an exam, since at this time you are dealing with all of the course material to date at once.)

Programming Memory   Studying your notes after the lecture, and even making a preliminary attempt to program them into memory, will save you an enormous amount of time and effort later on (see Chapter 6). It will enable you to prepare for exams in less time and with more confidence than if you put your notes away and then try to cram them all into your mind the night before the test.

Try to *avoid recopying* or typing out your notes after the lecture if possible. This is a very time-consuming process and *unless* your handwriting or your initial organization is terrible, this time would be better spent editing, underlining, organizing, integrating, and memorizing.

More will be said about the use of lecture notes in the next chapter, which is concerned with preparing for exams.

Summary

Lectures generally play a more important role in college than in high school courses; thus taking good lecture notes is important. Lectures can play many specific roles in a given course, and these roles should be clarified as soon as possible after the course begins. Note-taking from lectures is different from note-taking from reading in that it demands greater alertness and completeness. Students most commonly make errors of omission when taking lecture notes. The average student misses more than 40 percent of the material that the lecturer believes to be important. Such errors can arise from many sources, including misconceptions about the role of lecture notes, fatigue, overintegrating during the lecture, the speed or difficulty of the lecture, trying to write too much, and distractions. Errors of commission can also occur though they are less frequent. Notes should be read over (but preferably not recopied) after class for the purposes of editing, underlining, reformulating, organizing, integrating, and memorizing.

EXERCISES

1. List any three courses which you are now taking and identify, as precisely as possible, the role which lectures (and other classroom work) play in each course.

2. Do you ever commit errors of omission in your lecture notes (i.e., do you omit material which you actually *need* for purposes of the course)?

3. What factors contribute to these errors of omission? List any factors mentioned in Chapter 11 which apply to you.

4. Do you use your lecture notes properly? That is, do you edit? underline? reformulate concepts where needed? organize? integrate the notes with other material? try to program them into memory? In what areas are you deficient?

Evaluating Your Answers

1. Here is an example of a useful set of answers to this question:

Course	Role of Lectures
Psychology	presentation of new material and elaboration and expansion of text material
Government	entirely new material
Business Administration	rehash of book

Clearly lectures play a far more important role in the first two courses than in the last. The implications for action, as far as this student is concerned, are obvious.

2–4. The appropriate answers to these questions are easily determined by consulting the text of Chapter 11.

12. How To Prepare For and Take Exams

Before you can begin preparing for an exam, you must find out exactly what material will be covered by the test and, if possible, what types of questions (essay, multiple choice, etc.) will be given. If you are not sure, ask the teacher directly rather than guessing. Once this information has been obtained, four stages of exam preparation are recommended. In practice, the stages overlap somewhat and may be combined with one another.

Exam Preparation

Thorough Initial Study   It is crucial that you cover *all* (that means 100 percent) of the assigned material when you do your *initial* study. A surprisingly large proportion of students admit that they often fail to study (or to study thoroughly) all of the material that will be covered by their tests. The result is that they go into exams with definite *gaps in their knowledge or understanding*. They usually discover these gaps when they find themselves unable to answer one or more questions on their exams.

The justification given for these omissions is nearly always the

belief "Oh, he won't ask that." In many cases the cause of this belief
is simply a wish, that is, "I sure *hope* he won't ask that, because I
didn't study it."

The student may, of course, honestly think that certain portions of
the assigned material will not be tested because they are not important. This may be subjective (e.g., they are not important to him
personally); however, the student may also be objectively correct
—the material is *not* important. But it does not necessarily follow
that such material will be omitted from the exam. Sometimes
teachers choose questions solely to *avoid* asking the obvious. Remember that professors who have been teaching the same course for
many years often like to think up nonobvious questions in order to
make the tests interesting for themselves! Thus it is a poor policy to
omit from your *initial* study any part of the assigned material unless
you have a convincing reason for doing so (i.e., the teacher's own
statements, knowledge based on past exams constructed by the same
teacher, etc.).

Review Once you have read all of the assigned material at least once
(and understood it), you can *then* go back and review it selectively.
This review should be guided by the underlinings and margin notes
you have made in your textbook(s) and in your lecture notes (see
Chapter 5). That is, when you review, skim the parts not designated
as important and restudy the underlined parts; the amount of study
devoted to each should be proportional to the degree of importance
indicated.

This review should involve *active rereading* (see Chapter 7); specifically you should be actively integrating the course concepts with
each other as you reread. This should be easier and more efficient
than it was on the first reading, since by now you will have gained
some understanding of the individual concepts through abstract
reading and will have done some preliminary integrative reading. An
additional benefit of active rereading is that it will help program your
memory (see Chapter 7).

Exam Study Notes At some stage in your exam preparation you will
usually find it helpful to prepare exam study notes. Such notes serve
to organize the material in your mind, and provide a basis for testing
yourself later to see how effectively you have programmed the material into memory.

Exam study notes can be constructed to include varying amounts
of detail, depending on your own preference. However, it is recommended that the notes be roughly equivalent in detail to the "working notes" constructed from your readings (discussed in Chapter 5).

In fact, if your text material does not have to be integrated with the lecture material, your working notes can serve as exam study notes "as is." Otherwise, you will need to make a new set of notes which combine the material from both sources.

Exam study notes are expecially important in courses where you will have essay exams. If you simply try to memorize long, unorganized lists of facts taken from lectures and reading at random, you will not be able to construct a coherent essay. If you file the course material in your mind as a jumbled mess, that is exactly what will come out on the exam. To use a favorite analogy of computer operators: "Garbage in, garbage out."

Some students even make additional "subsets" of exam study notes consisting of detailed outlines of answers to likely essay questions which they have picked out by identifying major course themes. If you make such notes, be careful not to try to outguess the teacher by arbitrarily picking one or two themes while ignoring other possible questions.

If the course you are studying does involve mostly lists of concrete facts that have to be memorized (e.g., foreign language vocabulary), then simply making long lists, or putting each concept or word on a file card (with the correct translation, definition, or description on the back) may be adequate.

Programming Memory   Once you have read, understood, and organized the material to be tested, virtually *all* of your remaining efforts should be aimed directly at programming the material into your memory using the procedures described in Chapters 6 and 7. Hopefully, you will have started this programming well before the exam date so that you can avoid cramming and all of its disadvantages (see Chapter 6). The most generally useful method of programming memory, as noted in Chapter 7, is rehearsal. Your exam study notes can be used for rehearsal, since they will consist of an organized outline of the basic facts or concepts in the course.

If the exam you are studying for consists of problems (e.g., math, physics) your best method of "rehearsal" is to do the homework problems or problems at the end of each chapter on a regular basis. This will reveal whether you can integrate the formulas, principles, and theorems with concrete problems. If you cannot do the problems, see the course instructor, a teaching assistant, or a tutor at once.

When doing homework problems, be careful to avoid the procedure of skimming the chapter content, making a half-hearted attempt to solve the problems, looking at the answers (if given in the back of the book), and then trying to work backwards from the answers to see how they were arrived at. This method is useless for exam preparation since you are not given the answers to work back from during exams. This does not mean that you should avoid looking at the answers to homework problems to see if they are correct. But do so only *after* you have made a serious effort to understand the chapter on which they are based and to work through the problems fully. Then, if you have made any errors, you can identify their causes and try to avoid them on subsequent problems.

Exam-Taking

A common student complaint regarding the taking of exams is that it makes them nervous or anxious. Text anxiety is an important enough subject to require a separate chapter. Since this is primarily a motivational problem, however, the chapter on test anxiety has been placed in Part II of this book (see Chapter 17). The present discussion deals with the cognitive aspects of test-taking.

General Procedures   The first thing to do, after writing your name on the exam or any and all answer sheets, is to survey the exam quickly in order to determine how many parts and/or problems there are and the amount of time allowed for each.

This writer generally advises *against* glancing at the actual questions themselves in advance (*unless* this is necessary for the purpose of choosing which ones you will answer) for two reasons. First, if you do not immediately see how to answer most of them, you may go into a state of panic. This will prevent you from answering even the questions you can answer. Second, if you do know the material thoroughly, your subconscious mind may start making so many connections automatically that you may find it difficult to concentrate on answering any specific question. Reading all the questions first is like trying to program your mind with too many orders at once. (Of course, if you have found that these two problems do *not* apply to you, then ignore this warning.)

The exam survey should include a careful reading of all relevant *directions*, such as where to write your answers (on the test paper, on an IBM answer sheet, in a blue book, etc.), and how many of the questions you are to answer (e.g., all, one from each part, six out of seven, etc.).

Next you can begin to look at the specific questions. Before answering any given question you need to identify two things: (1) the *content* or subject of the questions (e.g., psychological defense mechanisms, the Civil War, the style of Victor Hugo, the physiology of the zebra, the law of gravity, etc.); and (2) the *operations* you are to perform on that content (e.g., list, describe, trace, compare, solve, define, outline, explain, etc.). Identifying these two aspects requires a *careful* reading of each question. There may be a tendency to rush headlong into your answer in order to reduce the anxiety you feel—a procedure which often leads to careless errors. This is especially common on essay exams (see below).

Let us now consider in more detail how to attack specific types of exam questions.

Essay Questions   There are three steps to follow after reading an essay question.

Outline.   First make a written outline of your answer. This is extremely important and should virtually never be omitted. The purpose of outlining is to help organize your essay into a coherent whole. The outline should specify at least the main points you will make, perhaps with a suggestion of the supporting facts you will mention. The points should, of course, be listed in some logical order.

Making an outline will help to prevent an error students commonly make on essay exams—plunging in feet first and frantically writing down everything that comes into their heads which is in any way associated with the subject in question. Typically the result is a disorganized jumble of unintegrated facts many of which have little or no relevance to the question asked. Sometimes an entire essay will be written on the wrong theme or subject simply because the student started writing without first thinking about what he was doing.

Making a preliminary outline also suggests how much time should be spent on each point. The more points to be made, of course, the less the time that can be devoted to each.

Write.   The second step is to write, following your outline. Some specific suggestions:

1. *Get right to the point.* Do not start with a long preamble, e.g., "This question asks about the causes of the American Revolution. I will answer this question from several points of view that will help to give us insights from various sources as to the causal factors that lead up to this great moment in the history of our country, namely the American Revolution." This is pure baloney, and the grader will simply assume you are writing it because you have nothing relevant to say on the issue.

2. *Use good handwriting.* One study found that essays written in

good handwriting were scored a *full letter grade higher* than exactly the same essays written in poor handwriting.[1] If the grader cannot read what you write, he will *not* assume that you must have written something relevant. He will grade you as if you have, in effect, written nothing at all.

3. *Do not give personal opinions* unless they are specifically asked for. Claiming that you personally agree with the lecturer's own views will not help you. He may not even be the one who grades the test, since this is often done by teaching assistants.

4. *Be clear.* This is important above all. Using big words (whose meanings you do not fully understand) will not impress the teacher nearly so much as pertinent ideas expressed in a clear language. Do not write sloppily and imprecisely with the view that "He'll know what I mean." An objective grader does not grade what he thinks you might mean, but what you actually say. If you write unclearly, he will assume your knowledge is equally fuzzy and grade you accordingly.

Edit.   The third step in essay writing is editing. Because you will typically be anxious and pressed for time, it is very likely that you will make at least some careless errors in your essay (such as writing a word you did not intend to write, omitting something you intended to say, leaving out a key word like "not," reversing or confusing two related facts, etc.). Take a little time, even if it's only a minute or two, to read over your essay after you have finished. In addition to finding errors and correcting them, you may come up with new ideas that you can add to your answer.

Multiple-Choice Questions   Some teachers deliberately try to trick you in multiple-choice tests, while others do not. In either case, however, you must read each question very carefully, since the correct answer may depend upon a single word (e.g., a "never," "always," "sometimes," "not," or some technical term similar to another term from which you have to distinguish it).

Usually one or two obviously wrong answers can be eliminated at once, which leaves you to decide among two remaining ones. Rather than wasting time agonizing over an item where you cannot decide right away on the correct answer, go on to the next item and come back to the difficult one later. Sometimes a later item will give you a clue as to the correct answer to an earlier one (and vice versa).

Some students have trouble with multiple-choice tests because they try to read too much into the questions; they assume that an

1. W. W. Farquhar, J. D. Krumboltz, and C. G. Wrenn, *Learning to Study* (New York: Ronald, 1960), p. 144.

answer that is obvious automatically must be wrong for that reason alone. While this can happen, the obvious answer is often the correct one. If your teacher is the tricky type, you will have to learn this (and how to cope with it) through experience.

Problem Tests   Tests which consist mainly or solely of problems (such as math, statistics, physics, etc.) should be approached just as you approach your homework problems, providing you have done your homework problems conscientiously (as described earlier). If you do the homework problems much more slowly than is allowed on a test, trying to do your homework faster may help train you for the pressure of test-taking. Some students like to pick an easy test problem first (if there is any choice) to raise their morale and self-confidence; others prefer to take the problems in order. Editing is important on problem-solving tests in order to catch and correct careless errors, especially computational errors.

Summary

Test preparation requires four interrelated stages: studying all of the material (including filling in gaps in your knowledge); reviewing the material actively; making exam study notes to organize the material; and programming the material into memory. Test-taking itself should begin with a careful reading of all general instructions regarding time limits, number of items, where to write the answers, etc. Then specific questions should be read with attention to both the content and the operations to be performed on that content. Essay questions should be answered in three stages: outlining, writing, and editing. Multiple-choice and problem tests also require careful reading and answering to avoid careless errors.

EXERCISES

1. Analyze your habits with respect to exam preparation. Do you study 100 percent of the material? review the material? organize the material with exam study notes? When appropriate, do you make outlines of answers to possible essay questions? Do you spend considerable time programming the material into memory?

2. In which area are you most in need of improvement?

3. Write the name of any course for which you know there is an upcoming exam. Write down a specific *study plan* for this exam. Describe in detail each step you will take.

Evaluating Your Answers

1–2. The answers to these questions depend on your personal context. Consult Chapter 12 for the principles involved.

3. The following are examples of good exam study plans. In each case, the student plans to review the material and to use exam study notes in a way that is well suited to the nature of the course. The plans also include programming memory.

> Review underlined points in readings and take notes (brief) on most important facts I might need to review or might forget. As I take the notes I will integrate information from the various books. Review lecture notes and integrate into reading notes if necessary. Review exam notes and start to test myself with questions.

> Since all material comes from lecture, I will rewrite my notes by condensing them and by developing main topics. From these notes I will rehearse and memorize as much as possible. I will later look at the first part of a topic and then say what I can on that topic.

> This involves integrating lecture notes with the various books covered. I will reread my lecture notes and books, making up organized exam study notes from important points covered in lecture, and examples of those points from the books studied. I will then decide on any themes or ideas which relate to all the books, and make a separate set of notes showing these relationships. I will then program my memory with both sets of study notes.

In this last set of plans the integration of the material around broad themes would be equivalent to answering hypothetical questions to prepare for broad essays.

Compare the three plans you have just read with the following ones, which as *total* plans of action are all *incomplete* in some way, although each contains some good ideas:

> For each time period in Roman history (1) Period of Kings to 509 B.C. (2) Republic, 509–27 B.C. (3) Empire, 27 B.C. to Fall, I will integrate notes from the lecture, text and supplemental reading material for the following topics in each period in Roman history: (1) general important events (2) religion (3) political (4) social (5) art (6) architecture (7) literature (8) science (9) military.

The preceding plan is a good example of how to integrate material to prepare for essay questions. But, the student apparently does not plan to review his underlinings in the books, nor has he mentioned programming memory.

> Integrate lecture notes with the reading material. Make an outline and fill in all empty spaces.
> Example:
> I. Apollo
>   A. Achievements
>   1.
>   2.
>   3.
>   4.
> I make this sort of outline up as I study and organize my facts; after studying I fill in the outline.

This plan shows a good example of making notes for an exam covering narrower abstractions. But it, like the Roman history plan, does not mention programming memory.

> Take my lecture notes and study them. If there is any question afterwards, I'll look it up in the textbook. Then I'll use the text for solid reading. Then when I feel I know the material, I'll get with one other person and we'll question each other.

In this last plan, the student does not mention making exam study notes.

13. Study Monitoring

In one respect this is the most important chapter you have read so far. Previous chapters discussed the proper mental operations to use when studying. But knowledge of these principles will be of little benefit to you if you do not actually use them. And to know if you are using them and to insure that you use them consistently, you must monitor.

What Is Monitoring?

The term *monitoring* was first used in a psychological context by Dr. Allan Blumenthal,[1] who defined it as "introspection directed to one's *methods* of mental functioning." Monitoring is not simply a matter of *observing* the mind's operations, however. "The monitoring faculty [also] operates as a supervisor, overseeing the . . . functions of consciousness." In other words, monitoring involves both the *identification* and *regulation* of one's own mental processes.

1. A. Blumenthal, "The Base of Objectivist Psychotherapy" (1969); reprinted from *The Objectivist* 8, no. 6 (June, 1969), pp. 6–10; no. 7 (July, 1969), pp. 4–9.

A crucial characteristic of monitoring is that it is volitional; that is, it is within your conscious control. It is important to emphasize the volitional nature of monitoring, because it means that you have the power to initiate and sustain, *by choice*, mental habits that are beneficial to your life and well-being and to change, *by choice*, mental habits that are inimical to your welfare.

Like any mental or physical skill, monitoring must be learned; it becomes easier, more efficient, and more effective with repeated practice.

Blumenthal's discussion of the concept of monitoring was given within the context of an article on psychotherapy. He demonstrated why monitoring was essential for mental health. What, then, has monitoring to do with study?

The purpose of study is to gain knowledge. But as noted in Chapter 2, the acquisition of conceptual knowledge is not an automatic process like visual perception. Successful studying requires that appropriate mental operations be performed on the material to be learned. The purpose of study monitoring is to insure that you are, in fact, performing these operations.

Studying actually requires a double or *split mental focus*. On the one hand, you need to be focused on the material itself (that is, on learning it). At the same time, however, you need to be constantly checking to see that you are actually performing those mental operations that produce learning. In short, you need to monitor your mental processes while studying. This does not mean you should monitor every second; this would obviously make it impossible to learn the material. Your monitoring faculty should operate somewhat like a night watchman inspecting a building who periodically turns on his flashlight to check up on things as he makes his rounds. (The flashlight in this analogy is your monitoring faculty.)

Now let us discuss some specific types of monitoring which should be performed while studying.

What To Monitor For[2]

Subject of Focus   The first thing to monitor for is the subject on which your mind is focused while you are trying to study. You

2.   I am greatly indebted to Dr. Allan Blumenthal, whose detailed explanations of monitoring in lectures and personal discussions contributed greatly to my understanding of the concept. This section is an application of Dr. Blumenthal's ideas to the subject of studying. I am solely responsible for the present interpretations, however.

should ask yourself, in effect: Am I focused on the subject matter of the book or on something else? You will frequently find that when you think you are studying, you are actually thinking about some other topic entirely (e.g., another academic subject, personal problems, an upcoming date or event, some recent experience, background noise or music, a frustrated wish, the time of day, future plans, etc.). Frequently the focus will be solely on "getting done" with the assignment rather than on what needs to be done to understand the material. Students frequently come home exhausted from hours of "study" when, in fact, they were actually studying only a small proportion of the time. Remember that time spent sitting down with a book in front of you looking at the pages but thinking about something else is *not* study time.

Get into the habit of catching your mind as soon as it wanders off the subject you are trying to study and bringing it back into focus immediately. The more you do this, the more you will be building up good study habits.

It should be added that there will be occasions when you are so fatigued or so preoccupied with an important personal problem that studying will actually be inappropriate and perhaps impossible. In such circumstances, you may find it advisable to stop studying and take time out to deal with your problem, to let your emotions die down a bit, to rest, or to engage in some relaxing activity. Observe, however, that even to know that you cannot study at a certain time requires monitoring.

Level of Focus Many degrees or levels of awareness or focus are possible to the human mind. As you wake up in the morning or fall asleep at night, you are close to a *sensory level* of awareness: you are "aware" but you are not quite sure of what. When you are looking at a tree or car or flower your level of awareness is *perceptual* to the extent that you are aware of these objects but are not thinking about their significance, meaning or interrelationship. When studying you should sustain a consistently *conceptual* level of focus. This involves understanding what you read (see Chapters 2–4).

A conceptual level of focus must be purposeful: the operations of your mind must be consciously directed toward a goal. Students frequently confuse thinking (purposeful mental activity directed toward gaining knowledge) with *daydreaming*, which is a passive, nonpurposeful, perceptual-level mental activity. In daydreaming, you are not directing your mind toward a goal but are letting it drift randomly at the mercy of chance associations.

Nonconstructive *fantasizing* is also frequently confused with thinking. Nonconstructive fantasies are those in which your mind is directed toward a goal but the choice of goal or the means of attaining it are based on your feelings or wishes rather than on a realistic appraisal of your actual capabilities and your circumstances, e.g., fantasies of impossible achievements. (Constructive fantasies, in contrast, do involve thinking. These may entail planning or mentally rehearsing future actions or contemplating the enjoyment to be derived from attainable future goals.)

A common symptom of being partially or totally out of focus is to find that when you complete a paragraph or chapter of material, you have no idea what you just read.

If you find that your mind is at too low a level of focus for effective study, then you should either raise it up to a more conceptual level each time you catch it drifting, or else get some rest or sleep and put off studying until such a time when you can remain in focus. Another alternative is to change to another book or subject. (If nothing seems to help, you should ask yourself such questions as whether you may have psychological problems needing attention; whether you really want to be in college at all; whether you have something more important on your mind; or whether your diet is deficient in some way, etc. Some of these issues will be discussed in Part II of this book.)

One warning: you can generally expect your average level of focus to decline as you become more fatigued. Thus, the longer you study, the more you should watch for it.

Type of Focus By type of focus is meant the particular context in which the reading is being done and the explicit and implicit purposes which you have when studying. Depending on the nature of the course and the material, you may be trying to learn concrete facts (Chapter 2), to understand a new concept (Chapter 3), to integrate material with other material (Chapter 4), to determine what is important (Chapter 5), to program the material into memory (Chapters 6 and 7), to listen to a lecture (Chapter 11), or to prepare for an exam (Chapter 12).

Whatever the context, monitoring will serve to insure that you are reading the passage (or listening to the lecture) from the point of view of the particular purpose (and therefore the particular emphasis) you require. It is, of course, perfectly valid to have several purposes in reading, but again you must be aware of what they are and whether the reading you are doing is helping to attain them. Sometimes you may find that you have too many purposes and are consequently becoming confused. Or you may find that you are doing the "right" thing at the wrong time, such as doing too much integrating during a lecture (see Chapter 11).

Implicit False Conclusions If you are not in the habit of monitoring, it is very likely that you will discover many little ways in which your mind "plays tricks" on you, or more precisely, ways in which you have trained it to play tricks on you when studying.

The most common trick of all is the knack of convincing yourself that you understand something when you do not. The way in which this habit develops is roughly as follows: You encounter some new concept or idea in your reading. You understand some part of it (perhaps only a very small part) and recognize this. At the same time you recognize that you do *not* understand some other aspect of the concept or idea and do not wish to expend the effort fuller understanding would require. You then focus on the part you do understand and push out of awareness the part you do not understand. All you are left with is the certain knowledge that you know part of the material and some fuzzy recollection that there is more that you do not know. What you then file away in your mind is: "I sort of know that" or: "I have the basic idea" or: "I understand it generally," etc. You may also promise yourself: "I'll come back to that later when I have more time." When you come back to it later you will probably recall only: "Oh, yes, I know that. I studied it before."

It is possible for a student to make this procedure virtually automatic by habitually skipping over material that is difficult and by habitually filing away very fuzzy approximations of the ideas or concepts he encounters (e.g., definitions with half the words missing; formal definitions with no idea of what the words mean; conclusions but not the reasons for them; facts or reasons but not the conclusions derived from them; one conclusion but not the other five; names of writers but not their ideas; dates but not what happened; formulas but not their meanings; etc.).

The filing of false conclusions can manifest itself in other ways. As noted earlier, some students in the physical and mathematical sciences have the habit of attempting homework problems before they understand the material. They do it by working backwards from the answers (if they are given) using a process of blind trial and error. When they "hit upon" a correct answer, they tell themselves that they understand the material, because they "got the problem correct." They fail to register *how* they got it correct and to recognize that such methods will not work on a test.

Do you have the habit of fooling yourself about your knowledge? One clue is doing poorly on tests and papers even when you "feel" you know the material. If you do have such a habit, you will find it easy to catch yourself reaching false conclusions when you start monitoring.

One way to avoid overestimating your understanding of new concepts or theories is to test your understanding of them systematically. A sample of pertinent questions you can ask yourself about each new concept or theory you encounter is shown on the left side of Table 2 below. These questions are based on the ideas presented in Chapters 3 and 4 and on some ideas proposed by Holt.[3] Not all of these questions are applicable to every idea you encounter, but if you cannot answer at least some of them with respect to each new concept or theory you study, you probably do not yet understand it.

The right-hand side of Table 2 illustrates this technique by answering the sample questions on the left with respect to the concept of "car." (This concept was originally defined in Chapter 2.)

False conclusions are not always about your understanding of the material. They may also occur with respect to your programming of the material into memory. Just because you recall some fact five seconds after you read it does not mean that you have programmed it into long-term memory (see Chapter 7).

One technique that encourages the filing of false conclusions about learning is going over the material too rapidly. Not only does this prevent the integrations you do make from "sinking in" (Chapter 6), it prevents you from fully realizing how much you are missing. Often students subconsciously speed up when they encounter difficult material (so they will not have to think about it) when they should, of course, slow down.

Subjectivism   Subjectivism in philosophy is the doctrine that objective reality does not exist, that "facts" are a matter of one's personal preferences, feelings, or whims. You do not have to accept this doctrine as a conscious philosophical conviction, however, in order to practice it, as a number of student habits indicate.

Wish-dominated appraisals of importance.   One way students rationalize not studying assigned material which they know they do not understand is by convincing themselves that some issue, idea, fact, or concept is not important (e.g., the "he-won't-ask-that" premise described in Chapter 12). They do not convince themselves through logical argument, but by letting their wishes override their judgment. One student, for example, convinced himself, despite the warnings of the teacher, that map learning (geography) was not really relevant to a course on Greek thought and so did not study it. When a map question was given on the exam, he missed most of it.

Arbitrary categorizations or reformulations.   The error of categorizing course material solely according to how you would *like* it to be categorized rather than in accordance with the purpose and

3.   J. Holt, *How Children Fail* (New York: Dell, 1964), pp. 136–37.

Table 2. Testing Your Understanding

Questions To Test Your Understanding	*Sample Answers Using the Concept of "Car".*
1. Can you define the concept or explain the idea in your own words? Can you do it clearly enough so that a friend who was not acquainted with the concept would understand?	1. A car is a self-powered conveyance with four wheels which moves people across solid, smooth surfaces such as roads.
2. Can you identify or point to some of the facts or phenomena on which the concept is based or the evidence which led to the theory, hypothesis, or conclusion? Can you explain the concept's derivation?	2. The concept of car is based on the existence of such vehicles as described in #1.
3. Can you think of specific examples of the concept or specific instances of the idea or phenomenon?	3. An example of a car would be a Ford, a Mazda, or a Datsun.
4. Can you recognize examples of the concept or instances of the phenomenon when you encounter them?	4. Yes, I know cars when I see them. (Point to one on the street.)
5. Can you identify relevant similarities and differences between this concept or idea and other, related concepts or ideas?	5. A car is similar to a jeep in that both have four wheels, but jeeps are mainly designed to cross rough surfaces. A car is like a motorcycle in that both are self-propelled, but motorcycles have only two wheels. A car is like a truck in that both may have four wheels and use smooth surfaces, but trucks are mainly for carrying freight (goods, etc.) rather than people.
6. Can you identify any implications or applications of the concept or idea?	6. What are the implications of continued growth in car use for such issues as: the need for fuel exploration? the Arab-Israeli conflict? the search for new types of engines?
7. Can you identify wider concepts which would include this concept? Can it be broken down into subcategories?	7. A car is in the general category of "self-propelled vehicles." Other vehicles in this category include jeeps, motorcycles, trucks, etc. (see #5 above). The concept of car itself can be broken down in several ways: e.g., by makes (Ford, Chevrolet, etc.), compact vs. non-compact, US vs. foreign made, piston vs. rotary engine, etc.

content of the course has already been mentioned (Chapters 3 and 4). While recategorization may promote understanding, if it is carried too far or is too personal, you may be marked off for it.

One student, for example, reported: "I find that I 'read' into the book things that aren't said there explicitly, and I can almost swear afterwards that what I 'read' into the book was really there all the time. This is occasionally a helpful device, but [goes] mostly against [me in] grades, tests, etc."

Personal agreement with ideas. While it is highly appropriate for you to evaluate what you are taught, it does not follow that you should *learn* only what you personally agree with. Every student must form the habit of *double bookkeeping* in school. On one side of your mental ledger should be: "What I know (or believe) to be true," and on the other side: "What my teachers, books, or some theory or writer says is true." For the purpose of exams, you must learn what is on the latter side even if you are convinced it is irrational. For the purpose of guiding your own choices and actions, you must obviously follow the former side.

Monitoring for Monitoring Not only should you monitor to see whether you are studying properly, but you should also check to see whether you are monitoring properly. This can be done by asking yourself periodically: "Am I monitoring? If so, what did I find? What did I do about it?" This is the method by which you acquire and sustain efficient study habits.

Training the Mind To Monitor

As noted earlier, you must train your mind to monitor effectively through repeated practice. You can do this by getting into the habit of regularly monitoring your mental processes during study. If you find that you need to correct your habitual level or type of focus you might begin by setting yourself specific *focus goals*, e.g., three minutes of studying without daydreaming, etc. You can make these intervals very short at first, if necessary, and gradually work to increase the length of time you can spend in full focus, simultaneously reducing the amount of time spent in pseudo-studying (day-dreaming, nonconstructive fantasizing, etc.).

When To Do Study Monitoring

Obviously you should do study monitoring when you first study text material. You should also do it when reviewing for and taking exams.

You should also do it during lectures and when programming your memory. Other occasions that call for monitoring are more related to motivation than to study methods and will be discussed in later chapters.

Summary

Study monitoring is one of the most crucially important skills the student can learn. Study monitoring entails the observation and regulation of your mental processes during study. You should monitor for: the subject of your focus; your level of focus; your type of focus; implicit false conclusions; various types of subjectivism; and whether you are monitoring or not. Effective monitoring requires training your mind through repeated practice.

EXERCISES

1. Before attempting this exercise be sure that you clearly understand Chapter 13. (Did you underline it? Put notes in the margins? Reformulate the main concepts in your own words?)

For this assignment you may choose any short chapter (or long passage) from any book in one of your current courses. Find a time and place to work without interruption. Then read the chapter or passage straight through (you may underline and make notes in the margins if you wish). As you read the chapter or passage, monitor the mental processes described in Chapter 13 (e.g., subject of focus, level of focus, implicit false conclusions, subjectivism, etc.). Jot down what you identify on a note pad as you go. When you are finished, indicate what you found when monitoring and the results of your monitoring.

Evaluating Your Answers

1. Here are some examples of good monitoring. Observe that these students not only *detected* (or anticipated) deficiencies in their mental processes while studying, they also made an effort to *correct* these deficiencies when they detected them. Remember: monitoring involves both the observation and the regulation of one's own mental processes. (Note: The monitoring reports below are only

excerpts from the considerably longer reports that most students give in answer to this question.)

> During the first few paragraphs, I was successfully concentrating, until I heard the phone ring . . . I began daydreaming that my friend was calling to ask me out. After somebody finally answered the phone, I had to go back to that point where I lost focus and change my reading from perceptual to conceptual . . .

> After 1 minute I was reading at the perceptual level. My mind was on another exam. Reread paragraph. After 4 min. was thinking about the time since I started reading. Reread paragraph . . .

> I had one big difficulty, I was so aware that I was being monitored (even though it was myself) I made a large conscious effort to concentrate on what I was reading. My mind focused on the subject being discussed. I didn't allow any other thoughts to be considered. I have never remembered and understood anything so well in my life . . .

The student above monitored so well from the beginning that there were no deficiencies to correct. Note also that he was able to detect a significant increase in his level of understanding over what it was normally.

> Near the end of the chapter, I found myself reading at the perceptual level because I wanted to get through it. I went back and reread it.

> Reading a paragraph with complicated words and definitions, I found I sort of skimmed over it believing I had read and understood the material until I caught myself and asked myself, "Why am I reading this?" I answered myself, "to gain skill in monitoring" and so returned to the paragraph, and now I understand it.

The student above failed to add that the purpose of gaining skill in study monitoring is to insure that one will, in fact, understand what one reads.

> Difficulty in focusing on subject—due to lack of interest. Thought about other courses, other homework. Occasionally at perceptual level . . . Attempted to pass

over complicated concepts; however, I forced myself to go back and reread and understand the ideas.

The following are examples of *incomplete* monitoring. These students detected deficiencies in their mental processes while studying, but they did not complete the process of monitoring by correcting these deficiencies when they observed them:

> Every 3 or 4 paragraphs I started daydreaming—next week-end, my girlfriend, the people sitting at my table in the library, etc. It seemed like I wanted to get done in a hurry. Near the end of the article I was reading at the sensory level. I put my head down on the table and fell asleep while I still had 2 or 3 pages to go.

> Most of the time my mind would go blank . . .

> I found myself daydreaming a lot and it was very hard to get through the article. I found the article very dry and boring and probably skipped over more terms than I should have . . .

> Listened to what the kids in my dorm were saying. Listened to who the telephone call was for. Wondered what was on TV tonight. Thought about seeing my fiancée tomorrow . . .

> About every 5 minutes I found myself reading at only a perceptual level. The material was very difficult. I found myself repeatedly trying to convince myself that I understood it when I really didn't. Twice when I really didn't understand the material I began daydreaming (girls) instead of making an effort to understand . . .

> I skipped over something I didn't understand and rationalized to myself saying, "There is no way he'll ask that on the test, and if he does ask it, I know enough about it to get by." In reality I knew nothing of the subject . . .

> . . . As I read further my eyes got heavy, and I felt very sleepy.

Part II
Study Motivation

14. Motives for Going to College

Why do you want to attend college? What do you hope to get out of it? Your answers to these questions will have important implications for your motivation to study while at college. Most answers fall into one of four broad categories.

Selfish Motives

The term *selfishness* is automatically associated in most people's minds with morally undesirable traits such as brutishness, ruthlessness, and lack of regard for the rights of others. The actual meaning of the term, however, is: *"concern with one's own interests."*[1] Such concern is an objective necessity of one's survival and well-being.

There is nothing in this definition that says one must disregard the rights of others in pursuing one's own interests; and, in fact, a ra-

---

1. Those who have doubts about the morality of being concerned with one's own interests and would like to study the issue in more detail are urged to read A. Rand, *The Virtue of Selfishness* (New York: New American Library, 1964).

tional man would not wish to do so, since it would be inconsistent with the desire to have his own rights respected.

Some students (e.g., those who see themselves as "idealistic") reject the idea of selfishly pursuing their own interests, because they see this as incompatible with bettering the society in which they live. Those who are troubled by this conflict should consider the following: first, bettering society *is* in one's selfish interest since one lives in society and is affected by it; second, *any* rational endeavor or career which one works at productively will benefit someone (even though that is not the moral justification of such work; see footnote 1). By producing goods or services which other people value, one makes trade possible. A trade is an exchange of values whereby each individual gives up something he wants less for something he wants more. Thus both parties benefit.

What selfish reasons could a rational student have for coming to college?

One such motive is the desire to *learn* and to *grow* in one's knowledge (both of oneself and of the world). A closely related motive is to satisfy one's *intellectual curiosity*. Since man needs to acquire knowledge to sustain his existence, it is valid for a person to enter college for these reasons even in the absence of firm career plans at the time of entrance. Definite career plans can be developed in or even after college as one gains greater knowledge of different fields of study and of the specific career alternatives that exist. In fact, a final career choice can even be made long after college, as in the case of middle-aged men or women who decide to switch careers. (College counselors, however, recommend that career planning begin as early as possible, preferably during the freshman year. Many colleges have "career development centers" or their equivalent which can help the student with this process.)

If the student does have a definite idea (or even a tentative idea) of what career he intends to pursue, he may find that college attendance is a *prerequisite to that career*. For example, nearly all of the professions (e.g., law, medicine, college teaching, psychology, engineering, etc.) require a graduate degree, and in order to get into graduate school one needs an undergraduate degree (and good grades as well). Other careers require at least a B.A. degree (e.g., many business and government jobs including officers in the Armed Forces).

The student should also recognize that as our society becomes increasingly technological, knowledge and learning are becoming increasingly important in all types of careers and occupations.

Some careers, however, do not necessarily require college degrees, e.g., artist, writer, professional entertainer or athlete, some business jobs (especially self-employed businessmen), etc. If you aspire to one of these careers, college may not be necessary, although it may still provide training that would help you in your career.

Two other types of benefits which an individual may obtain from college are *higher income* and *greater career flexibility*. The typical college graduate earns significantly more money in his working lifetime than does the average noncollege graduate, although there are wide variations around the average within both groups. Furthermore, having a college degree will give you a wider choice of careers than you would otherwise have. With a college diploma, you can enter almost any career that is open to noncollege graduates, but the converse is not true. Without a degree, many careers are automatically closed to you (e.g., the professions, many business jobs).

Selfless Motives

A second category of reasons for attending college involves motives opposite to those just described. These motives are selfless in that they involve the lack of a firm sense of one's own interests or values or the sacrifice of one's own values for the sake of others.

One example is going to college out of *duty*. Duty motivation is implied by such statements as: "I am going because my parents want (expect) me to"; "It's my obligation to obey them"; "I'm their only (or their last) child and they want me to be the first in the family to go." These examples imply that the motive for attending college is not that of the person going but that of his or her parents. The parents' moral justification for making this demand, without reference to the desires and goals of their son or daughter, is never specified.

Certainly there is no obligation to attend just because your parents raised you. Their caring for you was not a trade but an obligation which they undertook by choice when they decided to have you. Since children are born helpless, all parents assume this obligation until their children become adults. All the child owes in return is respect for their rights and appreciation for what they have done (if they have done a conscientious job). But he assumes no unchosen obligation (i.e., duty) to spend his life paying them back for what was his by right. Any parents who demand or expect this are not acting out of benevolence or out of consideration for their children. It is appropriate to want your parents to feel pride and happiness (if they have earned them), but not if these feelings are attained at your expense.

Another selfless motive is *conformity* to one's peer group: "I am going because all of the other kids went"; "I did not want to be left out"; "It was expected in our group"; "I wanted to be like my friends." Again there is no reference to any of the students' own motives (except fear), only to the values and expectations of others. The same applies to the motive of *prestige*, which is based on the desire to impress others (parents, friends, society, etc.).

In all of these cases, the focus is on what others want and value, not on what the student himself wants or values. And yet it is the student himself who actually attends college; it is the self who has to study; it is the self who must take exams and write papers; it is the self who graduates and goes on to pursue a career. Without a firm sense of self, of your own goals, values, and standards, you will find it very difficult to initiate and maintain the effort that college study requires.

These arguments should not be taken to imply that one should never listen to the advice of others (e.g., parents) when making a choice regarding college attendance (or major subject or career). Others can be of substantial benefit in providing you with *factual knowledge* concerning various contemplated alternatives (e.g., which college has the best reputation, types of jobs available in given occupational fields, etc.). It is *you*, however, who must evaluate this knowledge in the context of your own values and career aspirations. Others can also present arguments as to why college attendence is in your self-interest, but again you should not accept these arguments unless you are fully convinced by them.

Irrelevant Motives

A third category of motives are not necessarily inappropriate in themselves but are simply not relevant to college as such, for example attending for "social" reasons, including the desire to find a romantic partner or spouse. While social and romantic activities are an important part of an individual's life, when they constitute the sole or major motive for attending college the chances are that poor academic performance will result. The reason, of course, is that these motives offer no direct incentive for study.

"No" Motive

Often the student's answer to the question "Why did you come to college?" is "I don't know" or the equivalent (e.g., "I didn't know what else to do"; "Just to keep busy doing something"; "I couldn't think of anything better to do"). Students without well-defined goals seldom do very well in college since they have no incentive to expend the effort that study requires. During your high school years you live at home and are encouraged to study by parents; in college, motivation for study must come from within.

Some "motives" are equivalent to having no motive at all. For example, some students go to college simply "to have fun" or "to be happy." Such "psychological goals" do not specify what it is that the student regards as fun, but usually "fun" is doing whatever he "feels" like doing. Ironically, students who act on this premise do not have much fun. Psychological goals such as happiness cannot be achieved by seeking them "directly" (i.e., by acting on one's whims). Rather one must first identify what goals one wants to achieve in the world, determine how to go about achieving them, and then work to attain them. If the goals are chosen and pursued rationally, and are finally attained, the result will be happiness. The attainment of happiness in college requires that the student have specific academic goals in mind when he enters and that he work to achieve them while he is there. If he enters only with a vague *wish* to be happy, he will accomplish very little academically.

Thinking through your motives for going to college beforehand may save you a great deal of grief, conflict, and wasted effort later on.

I once met a very unhappy student who was flunking out of college for the third time. I asked him what he really wanted, and he replied that his greatest desire was to be a professional singer but that his parents had pressured him to attend college because they wanted him to enter a "respectable" profession like medicine. He experienced the conflict between their desires and his as an enormous feeling of apathy mixed with guilt—apathy because he could not accept their desires, guilt because he could not give up his own. The conflict was being subconsciously "resolved" by flunking out so many times that he would no longer be able to get into a college. Given his values and his conflicts, this student would have been better off not going to college in the first place (at least not then).

An increasing number of college and precollege students are finding it helpful to postpone or interrupt their education by taking a year off before or after starting college. This time is used to discover what types of jobs the outside world has to offer, to get actual work experience in different fields, to pursue long-neglected interests, and to think seriously about long-term goals. The effect of such an interruption is often a more mature, more highly motivated student.

How about you? Is going to college in your interest? Why?

Summary

The motives of most students who attend college fall into one of four broad categories: selfish motives pertaining to one's own rational interests and the benefits to be attained from a college education, such as learning, career facilitation, higher income, and greater career flexibility (motives in this category are crucial in arousing and maintaining the desire to study); selfless motives such as duty, conformity, and prestige where the values of others are guiding one's choices and actions; irrelevant (e.g., social) motives; and no clear motives or goals.

15. How To Cope with Fatigue and Boredom

Fatigue is the experience or sensation of reduced capacity for (mental or physical) work. All people, including students, feel fatigue at one time or another, since it is a normal and necessary accompaniment of work, i.e., of the expenditure of effort. Sometimes, however, fatigue is caused by conditions other than work—conditions which can be avoided or corrected.

Physical Causes

Some of the most obvious causes of unnecessary fatigue are physical in nature.

Insufficient (or Excessive) Sleep Adults require somewhere between four and ten hours of sleep (the average is about eight) to function efficiently and remain in good health. You will have to determine your exact need by trial and error. If you feel generally drowsy or grumpy or find it hard to get up in the morning, or get sick frequently, the chances are you are not getting as much sleep as you need.

If you think you do not have enough time to get your full sleep **145** quota, check to see if you are wasting any of the time you do have (see Chapter 10). A better organization of your activities may provide the extra time you need. If you cannot get all the sleep you require at night, consider an afternoon or early evening nap. As a last resort, you could try sleeping late on weekends.

If you suffer from insomnia, your doctor may be able to help.

Surprisingly, you can also become fatigued from too much sleep. If you spend too much time in bed, your body will become habituated to a low level of arousal and you will feel tired and sluggish even when you are up.

Improper Diet   Nutrition experts claim that breakfast is the most important meal of the day, since it provides most of the energy you draw on as the day progresses. Yet some people eat no breakfast at all. Others make the mistake of eating mostly sweets (e.g., a coke or coffee with sugar and a sweet roll). The sugar gives you some quick energy but burns out within an hour or two, leaving you drowsy and tired. Protein, on the other hand, burns more gradually and provides you with energy over a longer period. Milk, eggs, bacon, and some cheeses are good sources of breakfast protein.[1] If you hate breakfast foods, try at least eating a sandwich with meat in it. If you like to get it over with quickly, try one of the "instant breakfast" drinks.

Physical Illness   If you are just getting over or just coming down with a physical illness, you will have much less energy than normal and will need more rest and sleep than usual. If you become ill for an extended period (e.g., more than a week or 10 days) during the semester, you may find it advisable to drop one or more of your courses so that you do not become ill again trying to catch up. If you feel constantly tired, you could be suffering from some chronic condition which should be treated medically. When in doubt, see a doctor.

Inadequate Exercise   Some individuals find that their minds function very well with little or no exercise. Others, especially younger people, find that they feel more alert, energetic, and relaxed with regular daily exercise. Without it they feel restless and fidgety and have difficulty concentrating (although such symptoms may also indicate boredom).

Metabolism   With respect to the time of day when they feel most energetic, some individuals are "early morning people," others are "night people," and still others find they work best in the afternoon.

1.   For an extensive discussion of nutrition and bodily needs see A. Davis, *Let's Eat Right to Keep Fit* (New York: Harcourt Brace Jovanovich, 1970).

It is not clear to what degree this is a matter of habit, diet, innate physiological factors, or other causes. Even if you cannot modify your metabolism, however, you can use it to best advantage by concentrating your study hours during those periods when you are most alert.

It is also advisable to avoid eating big meals or taking alcohol before class or study periods since these can make you drowsy.

Do any of these physical causes apply to you? If so, what can be done to eliminate the problem(s)?

Psychological Causes

While fatigue is experienced as physical, its ultimate causes may be psychological in nature.

Boredom   When a task seems endless, mindlessly repetitive, unrelated to your interests and values, or does not hold or require your full mental capacity, it is experienced as boring. Prolonged boredom often leads to a feeling of fatigue. One way of determining whether your fatigue is caused by boredom or by some other cause is to switch (or contemplate switching) to an activity that does interest you and see whether or not you immediately feel more alert and energetic.

If you need to study material that you initially find boring and tedious, there are several techniques you can use to alleviate this problem.

Understanding.   A serious misconception exists among many students to the effect that "interests are either there or they aren't" and that there is nothing you can do about them. Underlying this is the implicit premise that interests are either innate or developed at a very early age and hence unchangeable after childhood. In fact, interests, values, beliefs, and knowledge are not inborn. They are acquired. One way in which interests are acquired is through familiarity. One can become interested in a specific subject through the process of examining it, learning about it, understanding it, and integrating it with one's other knowledge. Thus if an interest in what you are studying is not there to start with, it is possible to arouse it by the process of study, especially if this process is successful in leading you to understand the material. The more integrations (e.g., implications and applications) you can make on the material you study, the more interesting it may become.

(It must be stressed that understanding does not inevitably stimulate interest. One can understand something and still find it uninteresting, perhaps because one finds it illogical or because it has no implications for one's long-range goals or other areas of interest. However, understanding may at least increase your degree of interest over what it was initially.)

It is important to grasp the idea that interests can be *developed,* because if you function on the premise that "either you have them or you don't," you will wait passively for them to "push" you into study. Since no innate interests exist, you will wait a long time for nothing. On the other hand, if you make an effort to learn the material despite an initial lack of interest, you may find your interest increasing as you begin to understand it and become thoroughly absorbed in it.

Changing subjects.   If you become satiated with a particular subject, one way to arouse yourself is to switch to another one. You will find that you become bored at different rates with different subjects; thus how long you spend at each can be determined by personal preference providing you complete your assignments. When you come back to the original subject after switching to another, you may find renewed interest in it, and perhaps new insights as well.

Rest pauses.   As an alternative and/or a supplement to switching subjects, try rest breaks as a means of dissipating boredom. During these breaks, you can smoke, drink coffee, lie down, or do whatever you wish. Be careful not to make the break too long, however, or you will risk getting yourself entirely out of the "set" to study and may become drowsy or be distracted by some other activity. Try ten minutes as a first approximation to an ideal length of break.

Goal-setting.   In graduate school I was once confronted with preparing for a comprehensive exam in a specialty area in which I had little interest. To help get myself through the book, I set myself goals as to how many minutes I would take to complete each set of 10 pages and kept a graph to chart my progress. The excitement of trying to increase or maintain my speed kept me aroused enough to get through the book (and pass the exam!).

The biggest risk in setting goals of this type is that of sacrificing understanding to speed. Achieving your speed goals in such a case is useless because you will not understand the material when you are done (see the section on "Subject of Focus" in Chapter 13). If you set speed goals, then, be careful to maintain high quality standards (i.e., understanding) at the same time.

Small units.   Boring material is easier to tolerate if you study it in small doses. Some prefer to do their weekly assignment all at once in order to "get it over with" but there is a serious risk of doing just that without understanding what you read. On the other hand, there is less temptation to skip or to read at the perceptual level if your (self-generated) assignment is short.

Focusing on benefits of study.   Even if there are no immediate benefits to be gained from studying a certain subject, there is usually some long-range benefit involved, even if it is only getting your degree. You can help arouse yourself to action in such cases by reminding yourself of your reasons for taking the course (and attending college) and of the benefits of doing well and the penalties for doing poorly.

Longer-term solutions to the problem of boredom would include dropping one or more courses (and substituting others), changing majors, or even switching colleges (if there were reason to believe that this would result in more interesting courses).

Psychological Conflict   Another cause of fatigue is psychological conflict. Such conflicts involve the holding of two clashing, contradictory, or opposing premises or values. Psychological conflicts are partially or wholly subconscious and thus can be difficult to identify.

Many students, for example, are in conflict about being in college at all. The conflict would be of the form "I must go to college but I don't want to." Or the conflict may involve a choice of major: "I want to be an engineer, but my parents say I should go into premed." Or it may be an issue of wanting to do well but not feeling really up to it: "I must get all As and Bs but I just can't." Sometimes there is a conflict based on doubt about one's ability: "I must try my best but I don't dare, because it will mean I'm stupid if I don't do well."

Often a student whom one would describe as "lazy" and "apathetic" is not fundamentally opposed to the expenditure of effort but is simply scared to try hard for fear of being disappointed. Apathy can also result from discouragement resulting from past efforts that brought no results. The conflict amounts, in effect, to: "I should keep at it, but I'll never succeed."

A discussion of methods of identifying and resolving psychological conflicts is beyond the scope of this book. If you think you have serious problems of this type that you are unable to resolve, do not hesitate to seek psychological counseling. If counseling is unavailable, simply talking to a friend may help.

Purposelessness   Some students are always tired simply because they have no real goals, either in college or in life. A purposeless individual is bound to become bored in college, because he will have no reason for studying. This does not mean that one should have one's whole life planned out in advance at the time one enters college, but it is necessary to have at least some goal, even if it is only to increase one's knowledge. Some individuals who come with limited goals develop longer-range objectives as they learn more about career opportunities. Others find it more productive to drop out, go to work, and then return to college when they are more firmly decided on their career aspirations. Psychological and/or career counseling may help in this endeavor.

Do any of these psychological factors cause you unnecessary fatigue? What specific solution(s) can you think of?

Summary

Fatigue is the experience of reduced capacity for work. Physical causes of fatigue include insufficient sleep, improper diet, physical illness, inadequate exercise, and metabolism. A major psychological cause of fatigue is boredom. Boredom can be eliminated or reduced by techniques such as understanding and getting absorbed in the material, changing subjects when studying, rest pauses, goal-setting, studying small units of the material, and focusing on the benefits of studying. Psychological conflicts and purposelessness can also cause a student to feel fatigued. These problems sometimes require psychological or career counseling.

16. Blocks to Mental Effort

The two previous chapters discussed two sets of factors that can undermine study motivation: inappropriate motives for coming to college, and fatigue and boredom. This chapter will discuss additional factors that can block the expenditure of mental effort.

Misconceptions About Mental Effort

Mind Is for Emergencies   Some students fail to expend adequate mental effort because they have subconscious misconceptions about effort. One common belief, for example, is that *one's mind* (i.e., *one's conceptual faculty*) *is something that one uses only in emergencies* (e.g., the night before an exam), while the rest of the time one can drift along guided by one's perceptions of the immediate moment and one's feelings. The student who acts on this premise will find that work will pile up so fast that he will not have enough time to complete it when the emergency arises. How many students, for example, can read and understand all the material for even one hour-long examination (about four to eight weeks' work) by starting it the night before the exam? How many can write a good term paper in three days or even a week?

Ironically, if you function on the premise that your mind is only to be used in emergencies, you will find that it does not function very well even under those conditions. This procedure is equivalent to an athlete lounging on the beach, drinking beer, and smoking until the day before the big game and then trying to get in shape. Any athlete who followed such a procedure would perform very poorly. Just as your body does not function efficiently and skillfully without constant practice and training, neither does your mind. To quote Thomas Edison (perhaps America's, if not the world's, greatest inventor):

> It is because they do not use their thinking powers that
> so many people have never developed a creditable
> mentality. The brain that isn't used rusts. The brain that is
> used responds. The brain is exactly like any other part of
> the body: it can be strengthened by proper exercise, by
> proper use. Put your arm in a sling and keep it there for a
> considerable length of time, and, when you take it out,
> you find that you can't use it. In the same way, the brain
> that isn't used suffers atrophy.[1]

Desire for Immediate Benefits   Another common misconception held by students is that there is no point in studying unless the course(s) you are taking yields some *immediate, directly perceivable benefit.* Such students often prefer the latest "relevant" courses—even though what is "relevant" today may be irrelevant tomorrow.

It is appropriate to want benefits from your college courses (see Chapter 14), but not all benefits are immediately obvious and not all of them accrue right away. Some courses may only be a prerequisite to getting your degree. Others may help teach you how to write or think. Still others may be helpful in preparing you for more advanced courses. Occasionally a course may open up a new area of knowledge for your consideration as a career or as an avocation. Or it may simply provide you with a store of knowledge to be used years later (e.g., a foreign language course might help you in foreign travel). Even courses which teach nonsense can be indirectly useful. By identifying what is wrong with the ideas you are being taught, you can clarify your own thoughts on the subject. Nearly all courses can be of some benefit to you. It is up to you to discover what they are.

1.   D. D. Runes, ed., *The Diary and Sundry Observations of Thomas Alva Edison* (New York: Philosophical Library, 1948), p. 167.

Determinism   A third misconception that can inhibit study motivation is the doctrine of *psychological determinism*. This is the theory that everything a person thinks, feels, or does is determined by forces outside his control, that man is the powerless victim of the forces which impinge upon him and has no freedom of choice with respect to thinking, values, or actions. Determinism asserts that man is a passive responder to stimulation and is incapable of purposeful, self-generated action.

Not many students would consciously accept the doctrine of psychological determinism,[2] but there are many who hold views which indicate that they have accepted it subconsciously.[3] For example, when a student argues that he performs poorly in a certain subject because "I just can't do math (French, English, history, science, etc.)," often his underlying premise is that he does not possess enough "innate ability" to understand these subjects. While it is probable that individuals are born with different mental capacities (potentialities), it should be stressed that *there is as yet no known method of measuring innate mental capacity* (e.g., intelligence). All intelligence tests measure the number of concepts you *now* know or how well you can integrate and use these concepts. All concepts, however, are acquired after birth, through learning. They are not inborn. Thus what is important is not what innate capacity or potential you start with, but how fully you utilize and develop the capacity you have. Many students who claim not to have enough innate ability to understand a certain subject do not suffer from a lack of innate capacity so much as from apathy stemming from the *belief* that such understanding is beyond their control.

There are other ways in which students accept the doctrine of determinism subconsciously—"I just can't study because of the noise"; "This teacher is so mixed up nobody can understand the course"; "I just can't seem to get to class on time"; "I just don't have time to do all my work"; "I'm just the nervous type—I panic in exams"; "I'm just lazy."

2.   For one, it can be observed by introspection that one can choose to use one's mind or not; but more fundamentally, the doctrine of determinism leads to insuperable self-contradictions. For example, how can the determinist claim that the doctrine of determinism is true and at the same time argue that he was compelled to believe it (and to say that he believes it) by forces outside his control?

3.   I am indebted to Dr. Allan Blumenthal for identifying the fact that individuals can hold the doctrine of determinism subconsciously. I am entirely responsible for the present interpretations and examples, however.

All of these statements indicate an implicit acceptance of the fact that certain actions, traits, or conditions are out of one's control, that one is at the mercy of innate or environmental factors over which one has no influence. While this is sometimes the case, more often it is a matter of passively accepting conditions that one *does* have the power to change. For example, if there is too much noise where you study, have you considered studying somewhere else? If a teacher is, in fact, mixed up, how can you make the most of the situation by preparing yourself thoroughly? If you come to class late because of oversleeping, could you go to bed earlier or use a better alarm? If you are pressed for time, can you organize your time better or undertake fewer activities?

If you are anxious during tests, is it because you are "just the anxious type," or could it be that you are simply not properly prepared (see Chapter 17 for details)? Are you actually "just lazy" or are you simply not clear on your life goals or perhaps afraid of trying (see below)?

Try to think of all the things relevant to your study methods, study environment, and study motivation that you have implicitly assumed were "determined" or out of your control. You may be surprised at how many of them you *do* have the power to change!

Emotional Blocks

Often as a result of or in addition to such misconceptions as we have just considered, the student will suffer emotional problems that undermine his ability and willingness to study. Since such problems may be very complex and may require psychological counseling, no complete discussion of them can or will be given here. Rather some of the most common problems will be discussed briefly and some techniques for (partially) coping with them described.

Fear   One common emotional problem is *fear of failure.* Some individuals, for example, are more concerned with avoiding failure than they are with achieving success. To avoid failing they may set themselves goals so low that they could not possibly fail to reach them, or, conversely, they might set goals so ridiculously high that no one (including themselves) could expect them to be reached. Or they might take refuge in apathy by convincing themselves that they do not care about anything. Without commitment there is no obvious disappointment, and without effort there is no significance to the failure. ("If you fail without trying, no one can say you are stupid or mediocre.") Some students avoid failure by taking pride in their "aspirations" or "potential," using these as a substitute for actual achievements (e.g., "I could be an A student if I really wanted to").

(It should be noted that none of the above defenses actually work, because, while you can temporarily "fool" your conscious mind, you cannot fool your subconscious. Implicitly you will know that you are avoiding commitment out of fear and will experience disappointment with yourself and lowered self-esteem.)

Fear of failure almost inevitably involves some wrong implicit evaluation of the meaning of failure (e.g., "It means I'm stupid, incompetent, no good, helpless," etc.) and/or an irrational standard of success (e.g., being omniscient; never making an error; always being the best; matching the achievement of some brilliant acquaintance or even of some fictional character in a novel).

There are also students who fear success! Typically they have become "comfortable" over the years with their view of themselves as "someone you cannot expect too much from." Such individuals may fear success because it would imply that they are capable of standards of performance which they could not attain consistently. Ultimately, they fear success because they fear that failure might follow.

Coping with fear of failure requires, among other things, a clear recognition of the following: (1) avoiding the pursuit of realistic goals will result in one's never achieving anything that one can be proud of; (2) letting one's feelings rather than one's rational judgment dictate choices and actions will, in itself, make one feel helpless, "determined," and out of control and will lower one's self-esteem; and (3) the consequences of failure are rarely so disastrous as one anticipates, especially if one takes care not to draw invalid, emotionally-based conclusions from the experience. (Coping with actual failure will be discussed in detail in Chapter 18.)

Anger Another emotional state that interferes with effective study is anger. Anger can be a response to the frustration brought on by an injustice, a moral betrayal, or the blockage of some goal the individual is trying to achieve. The precipitating cause may be an argument with a romantic partner, roommate, friend, or relative; some action taken by a teacher or the school administration; or something one did or failed to do oneself (e.g., study for or do well on an exam). Sometimes the events or conditions which caused one to become angry can be changed. For example, a student who feels he was treated unjustly by a teacher could appeal directly to the teacher and attempt to get him to correct the injustice. (If you do this the best approach is to be firm but polite. If you are hostile and obnoxious, he will resent your tone and be unsympathetic. If you are cringing and apologetic, he will conclude that you are not confident of your position and will not take your complaint seriously.) If the teacher gives you no satisfaction, you can always go to the chairman of the department in which the course is offered. If this fails, the next step is the dean of the college, and then the president or vice president of the college. There may be other methods of appeal in your college in addition to these.

Some students get angry at other people for circumstances which they have actually brought about themselves, e.g., accusing the teacher of making up an unfair exam, when in fact all the teacher did was to fail to ask the questions the student "hoped" he would ask. The real solution in such a case is to prepare for the exam more thoroughly the next time (see Chapters 12 and 18).

Guilt   Guilt often undermines study motivation. Guilt results when one believes one has violated some moral value or acted against one's better judgment. Sometimes guilt is largely *unearned*, as in the case of one young lady who started off each semester very well but then began to feel guilty when her friends did not do as well as she. To reduce the guilt she allowed her performance to decline toward the end of the semester. This student, without realizing it explicitly, felt guilty about what were actually virtues, not vices. Similarly there are some very compulsive students who feel guilty about engaging in any leisure activity; they do not realize that students need periods of rest and recreation to recuperate from past work and to refuel themselves psychologically for future study.

Some guilt, however, is *earned*, as when a student claims "I should have studied more for that exam" and, in fact, he should have. Or the student may be wasting his time (and his parents' money) by attending college when he is getting nothing out of it. The solution in these cases is to modify your guilt-producing actions as quickly as possible.

Depression   A very common emotional state that nearly all students suffer through at one time or another is *depression*. Depression occurs when one believes that one has lost (or will lose) some important value (including the value he puts on himself). The precipitating cause of depression can be rejection or severe criticism by friends, romantic partners, parents, or others; doing poorly on a test or in a course; failing to make firm decisions about anything, including one's own plans for the day; or failing to follow through on decisions once made. The ultimate causes of depression may involve errors the individual makes in processing and evaluating such events and the wrong conclusions he draws from them. (For example, an individual who is rejected by his or her romantic partner may conclude that he or she is worthless and undesirable. The error lies in basing one's self-esteem on the reactions of others.)

While treating depression is beyond the scope of this chapter, one technique you may find helpful is to *focus on the future* in the face of depression. Especially important is the development of specific plans of action to alleviate the present situation (e.g., see Chapter 18) and reminding yourself that things were not always and will not always be like they are now.

In dealing with depression it is also important to distinguish between those things you can control and those you cannot and to focus on the former when formulating plans of action.

If you suffer from frequent, prolonged or severe depression do not hesitate to seek psychological counseling.

Emotions and Study Mood

There will be many times when, owing to emotional conflict, you will not be in the mood to study. Often the best solution is simply not to study under such circumstances. At other times, however, studying may actually improve your mood. For example, if you have done poorly on a test, getting right down to work at that course may give you new confidence that the difficulties can be overcome (see Chapter 18 for details). Also studying may help you to forget worries and problems about which nothing can be done at the moment.

Do any of the above blocks to mental effort make it difficult for you to study? What, specifically, can be done to remove them?

Summary

Study motivation can be undermined by various types of misconceptions and by emotional problems. For example, a student might hold the implicit premise that his mind is to be used only in emergencies; or he might be wrongly demanding immediate, visible benefits from all of his courses; or he might subconsciously accept the doctrine of psychological determinism. Emotional difficulties that can impair the desire and willingness to study include fear of failure, anger, guilt, and depression. If such states are severe and/or prolonged, psychological counseling is advisable. Such emotions may make study impossible, although one's mood may sometimes be improved by study.

17. How To Cope with Test Anxiety

Every student has experienced test anxiety at some time in his life. Anxiety is not only unpleasant in itself; it can lead to mental paralysis and poor test performance. In order to cope with test anxiety, however, one must first understand its nature and causes.

Since the subject of anxiety is a very complex one, it will not be possible to deal thoroughly with all aspects of it here. This chapter will be limited to identifying some principles and techniques which you may find helpful in coping with test anxiety.

The Experience of Anxiety

Anxiety has both psychological and physical manifestations. Psychologically, to feel anxious is to feel afraid, uneasy, nervous, worried, tense, uncertain, helpless and (partly or wholly) out of control. Physically, anxiety may entail one or more of the following symptoms: heart palpitations, butterflies in the stomach, indigestion, diarrhea, nausea, vomiting, dizziness, faintness, weakness, rapid breathing, dryness of the mouth, sweating (especially of the palms), muscle tension (in the forehead, neck, shoulders, abdomen, etc.), **159** headaches, restlessness, jumpiness, shaking, trembling, itching, cramps, blurred vision, runny nose, hiccuping, pallor, loss (or increase) of appetite, etc.

All of these physical symptoms can occur for reasons other than anxiety, but if you feel one or more of them mainly when you are anticipating or taking a test, the chances are that they are caused by test anxiety. If your physical symptoms are particularly severe, your doctor may be willing to prescribe tranquilizers to relieve them.

Some students get so upset over their symptoms that they become even more anxious than they were originally. You can limit this "secondary anxiety" (anxiety about anxiety) by recognizing that these symptoms are normal accompaniments of anxiety and by remembering that they will subside when you leave the test situation. (If your symptoms are very intense and/or prolonged, consult a counselor or physician.)

The Causal Sequence Leading to Anxiety

Anxiety is basically a response to perceived *threat*. More precisely, it is the form in which you experience a perceived threat to your well-being or to your self-concept (self-image, self-esteem). At least three conditions are required for a person to experience anxiety: (1) the individual must perceive an object, situation, outcome, idea, etc. as threatening his self-concept or his values; (2) he must perceive a need to cope with the situation by acting to preserve his self-concept or his values in the face of this threat; and (3) he must be uncertain as to what the outcome will be, i.e., as to how effectively he will be able to deal with the situation.

In the case of test anxiety, the object is, of course, the test itself. The perceived need is to perform on the test in a way that measures up to one's standards and aspirations. The uncertainty results from not knowing what the questions will be and not knowing how well one will be able to answer them.

Eliminating the Causes of Test Anxiety

The analysis just given implies three possible strategies for reducing or eliminating anxiety, namely, changing the situation, changing one's aspirations or values (or one's estimate of what the test means), and changing one's estimate of one's ability to cope with the test.

Changing the Situation   Since the test is the precipitating cause of the anxiety, obviously not showing up for the exam or dropping the course would be one way to eliminate it. But this is not very practical if one values a college education, since such action, if practiced consistently, would lead to flunking out of school. Thus the solution to test anxiety must be found elsewhere.

Changing One's Appraisal of the Test Situation   Students can experience intense test anxiety because they put too much significance or the wrong kind of significance on a test. For example, a student might subconsciously "reason" as follows: "If my grade on this test is low, my course grade will be low, which will ruin my grade average for the semester, which will hurt my cumulative grade average, which will mean I won't get into graduate school, which means I can't enter the field I want. My God, my life will be ruined if I don't do well." The student does not literally reason out such a conclusion; if he did, he would see its absurdity. Rather he reaches it subconsciously, by means of emotional generalization. Rarely, if ever, does any one test actually have the significance indicated in the above example.

Some students draw exaggerated conclusions about what a test grade will mean about them as a person. They may see it as indicative of their intelligence, so that if they do poorly it means they are stupid, incompetent, and worthless. They fail to realize that course exams indicate only one thing: how much you know at a given time about a particular topic. This depends on the amount of studying you have done and on the correctness of the methods of study you have used. While intelligence helps, it is rarely the most important factor in determining grades.

Occasionally a student will consider writing a perfect test to be a "must" and condemn himself unmercifully for not getting 100 percent every time. Such a student is, in effect, judging himself by a standard of omniscience; he is failing to recognize that all of his knowledge has to be acquired and that some errors in the process of learning are inevitable. Learning from your mistakes is far more important than how many you make to start with.

Many students set aspirations for a test (or course, or their grade average) that are unrealistic in view of their past performance, present study methods, and the amount of work they put into study. Thus they necessarily feel inadequate to the task of living up to these aspirations. This does not mean that high aspirations are wrong, but rather that one's aspirations should be set realistically, taking into account one's known capacity at the time (based on past experience).

If one is dissatisfied with one's present level of performance, one can set a goal to *improve on it* each time so as to work up to a higher level of performance gradually.

One of the major reasons that students set unrealistic aspirations is that they base them on the demands and expectations of others rather than on their own thinking. For example, a student may decide that he simply *has to* do better than his roommate or his friend down the hall, or do as well as his parents say he should, or do better than his older (or younger) brother(s) or sister(s). In addition to producing aspirations that may be totally unrealistic in view of one's own personal situation (ability, major, college, curriculum, teacher, time available, etc.), allowing others to control one's life in this way does put one genuinely out of control. This in itself will cause anxiety.

What does the foregoing imply for coping with (reducing) test anxiety? It implies that you should check to see that you are putting the test in its proper perspective. Are you misinterpreting its significance? Overestimating its importance? Are your aspirations unrealistic? Are they your own?

Think of it this way: a test is a test. It is not the end of the world or the last judgment.

Enhancing One's Ability To Cope with Tests   A very frequent complaint among students goes something like this: "When I went into the test I knew the material cold, but then I got so nervous my mind went blank." I have questioned many students who claimed to have experienced this problem and have found *in most cases the student's mind was blank not only during the test but before the test as well.* The anxiety in such cases was the *result rather than the cause of their poor performance.* While they claimed that the sequence of events was: "Knew the material before the test—felt anxious—went blank," the actual sequence was: "Did not know the material before the test—realized this fully as soon as I tried to answer the questions—felt anxious."

It is important not to assume too readily that your "blank-outs" on tests are the result of anxiety, since such a conclusion may make you very passive about studying—"Why study, since my mind will go blank during the test anyway?" Before concluding that you went blank on a test, ask yourself whether you were not (at least partially) blank before the test began.

If you discover that you did not know the material thoroughly, the solution is of course to study more effectively in the future. The best way to convince yourself that you can cope with a test is to know the material "cold" and to know that you know it. You can only know this if you have used the appropriate methods of study in the course (see Part I of this book).

This is not to deny that genuine blanking out occurs. It does. But I believe that it is far less prevalent than is commonly supposed. For example, a student once came to my office after doing poorly on a test claiming that he really knew the material and that his problem was blanking out due to anxiety. I went over his test paper in detail and noticed that 80 percent of his errors were on the reading material, while only 20 percent were on the lecture material, and yet half the exam questions were from the reading and half were from the lectures. If his problem were solely one of test anxiety, he should have made an approximately equal number of errors on both types of question. The solution to this student's so-called anxiety problem was to study the reading material more thoroughly.

If you have a genuine problem of blanking out when you really know the material, one solution is to "overlearn" it before the exam. To "overlearn" means to rehearse and practice the material well beyond the point at which you first think you have mastered it. The purpose of this is to make the connections in your mind more automatic so that you can "call out" the relevant answers almost without thinking when you need them. Self-testing or having another person test you after you have studied thoroughly may help you to accomplish this. Knowing that you can answer any reasonable question that is put to you will give you confidence which should transfer to the actual test situation.

Do you suffer from test anxiety? How severe? What is the most important cause of this anxiety? Is inadequate test preparation an important factor?

Coping with the Effects of Anxiety

Even when anxiety does occur, it need not upset your psychological equilibrium nor impair your performance on the test. Below are described some specific ways in which test anxiety can disrupt performance and steps you can take to prevent such disruptions.

Resisting the Temptation To Rush or Escape There is often a tendency to rush when you are anxious, not just because of the time pressure but because you want to escape the tension by "getting it over with" (especially if you feel you are not doing well). Rushing often leads to careless errors, such as plunging into an essay without outlining or thinking, reading multiple-choice questions incorrectly, and making computational mistakes on problem questions (see Chapter 12). While you may not be able to help feeling anxious, you can resist acting on this feeling by identifying why you feel like rushing, reminding yourself that rushing will hurt your performance, and making an effort to slow down.

A related motive for rushing is the fear that if you do not get down everything you know right away, you will forget it. While this is unlikely to happen, such forgetting can easily be prevented by jotting down facts or ideas as they occur to you in the margin of your test paper for later reference.

Sometimes the desire to rid oneself of the tension involved in test taking goes beyond the desire to rush through it. One may feel like just getting up and leaving without even trying to finish. One student I knew found it helpful at times like this to hold firmly in her mind the alternative to obtaining a college degree. For her the alternative to college was the mindless drudgery of some routine clerical job without any chance for growth or self-development. Focusing clearly on this option in times of stress eliminated any temptation to run away from exams or from the pressures of study.

Resisting the Desire To Give Up   Some students will not tolerate the tension of trying for a goal when the outcome (success, failure, etc.) is uncertain, and so after encountering difficulties in answering some of the test questions, they simply give up. Since nothing is at stake when one stops striving for one's values, there is no tension. But remember: there is no achievement either!

Often giving up is preceded by a process of *emotional generalization* that goes something like this: "My God, I can't answer the first question. I must have studied all wrong. How stupid! I must be an idiot. I probably won't get any of the questions right and will flunk the exam. This course is a complete loss. So what's the use of trying?" It is obvious that the student's conclusions go far beyond the objective facts of the situation, namely the fact that he could not answer the first question on the exam. Such emotional generalizations can be actively resisted by making sure to *limit your conclusions* to what is objectively implied by the facts of the situation. For example, missing one question does not mean you will fail. Doing poorly on one exam does not necessarily mean that your chance for a good grade in the course is lost.

Giving up may also be a way of punishing yourself for being "stupid" (for not knowing all the answers). Or it may stem from the fear of being proven "stupid" if you try and then do poorly (see Chapter 16).

You can resist the temptation to give up prematurely by reminding yourself of several pertinent facts:

—important values are never attained without effort and struggle;

—doing well on the test (and in the course) may help you to attain other important values;

—giving in blindly to your feelings will make you feel guilty, out of control, and lower your self-esteem;

—refusing to sacrifice your feelings to your judgment (such as by deciding to persist despite your anxiety) will give you a sense of pride and self-satisfaction;

—if you keep trying, you may find that you can answer more questions than you thought you could (assuming you have done some studying for the test);

—doing poorly on a test does not prove you are stupid or incompetent but only that you did not know that material.

Avoiding Indecision   Anxiety entails uncertainty, and uncertainty can lead to vacillation during a test. For example, you might feel unable to decide which of two answers to a multiple-choice question is correct, or which of two essays to write, or which of two ways to go about solving a problem. Indecision wastes time, which can result in your having to rush through the remaining questions—a procedure that can lead to careless errors.

Sometimes indecision is due to your not having read the questions carefully enough, but it can also be due to the fact that you have only partial knowledge of the material being tested or of ways to apply it to the questions being asked.

In the case of a conflict between two essays, it may help to focus more clearly on the extent of your knowledge by making a brief outline of *both* essays and then deciding which subject you know more about. Even if this does not work, always put a definite *limit* on your decision time; once that time limit is reached make a firm decision and follow through on it. The time limits themselves will have to be set by you, but as a rough estimate on an hour-long exam, 1–2 minutes is the most you should usually spend on any multiple-choice question (you should spend far less on most of them), and 2–4 minutes should be the maximum for deciding between two essays.

Another possibility is to skip the decision altogether for the time being and to come back to the problem question(s) after completing the rest of the test. Often you can gain a new perspective in this manner and your decision upon returning to the questions can be made rapidly. (Once you have studied the questions, your subconscious mind will continue to work on them even while you are consciously focused on other items.)

Focusing on the Test Instead of Your Feelings   One reason that anxiety can disrupt test performance is that it distracts your attention from the test questions. Your mental focus can be so dominated by "worry" (about how you are doing, how hard it is, how things will come out, how disastrous the whole situation could be, etc.), that there is no room in your mind left for the test itself.[1]

While you may not be able to help feeling some anxiety on the test, you can prevent it from dominating your thoughts by making a conscious effort to focus on the *test questions* rather than on the anxiety you feel. Instead of sitting passively in a state of panic, tell yourself: "OK, so I'm anxious; now let's see if I can answer these questions." In short, make a conscious effort to maintain a consistent *task focus instead of a worry focus*. This in itself may reduce your anxiety, since you will be trying to cope actively with the situation rather than relinquishing control to an emotion.

Have you ever tried any of the above methods of reducing test anxiety? Which do you think will work best for you?

Summary

Test anxiety is a common experience among students. Psychologically, it entails a feeling of being helpless and out of control; physically, it may involve numerous symptoms including sweating and muscle tension. Anxiety is the result of threat; the individual perceives that there is an important value at stake, which he must act to gain or keep, and he is uncertain of his ability to cope with the situation. To cope with test anxiety one can attack its causes by modifying one's estimate of the meaning of the test or one's value standards, or by increasing one's ability to cope with the test by studying more effectively. One can also anticipate and counteract effects of anxiety such as rushing, giving up, indecision, and worrying.

1. J. Wine, "Test Anxiety and Direction of Attention," *Psychological Bulletin* 76 (1971), pp. 92–104.

18. How To Cope with "Failure"

The best time to read this chapter is just after you have "failed" a test. For the purposes of this discussion, the term *failure* will be used to refer to receiving *any* grade lower than what you consider acceptable. While some students consider anything above an F to be acceptable, others are only satisfied with Cs or higher. Still others consider Cs to be inadequate, and a few treat anything less than an A as equivalent to failure. (More will be said about setting rational standards of success later in this chapter.)

The Emotional Aftermath of Failure

As a result of failure on a test, you may feel stunned, shocked, frustrated, unhappy, dissatisfied, discouraged, upset, disgusted, disappointed, or depressed. If you firmly believe you should have done better, you will feel guilty and angry at yourself or the teacher (or both). You might even call yourself "stupid" and begin to wonder whether you "have what it takes" to do well in college. You may experience self-doubt and feel anxious about the future. If everything seems hopeless, you may feel like crying.

Some students react to failure with rage. They swear, pound their desks, rip up their tests, throw them away, and refuse to think about the subject any further.

While this writer is sympathetic to the unpleasant feelings generated by failure, you must recognize that neither these emotions nor any thoughtless actions taken in response to them will help you in the slightest to cope with the original problem—namely, the failure itself. Most unpleasant emotions can be tolerated providing there is some reasonable hope for improvement. The source of such hope is the conviction that, by identifying the causes of past failures, future failures can be avoided.

The first step in coping with failure, therefore, is to diagnose its causes.

Failure Diagnosis

Students often conclude that their failure was due primarily or entirely to a lack of sufficient intelligence or academic aptitude (or lack of aptitude for a particular type of subject matter, e.g., languages, mathematics, etc.). This does cause failure, but much less often than is commonly believed. How many students who did poorly on a test can honestly say that they could not have done better? Sometimes the *belief* that one does not have ability in a certain subject leads one not to try very hard; the poor results then seem to confirm the original belief, when, in fact, not trying very hard is the real cause of the problem.

If your problem is not one of inadequate ability, then where does it lie?

Examine the Test   The main source of clues in diagnosing failure is the test itself. Look especially for *patterns* in your errors. For example, did you miss more of the questions on the lecture material than those on the reading material? Did you do more poorly on the questions involving one particular subject or book than on those involving another subject or book? Did you do better or worse on essays than on multiple-choice items? Were your essays relevant to the questions asked? Did you make any careless mistakes? Were there some concepts or ideas on the test that you had never heard of before? Was your understanding of some of the concepts hazy? The answers to these questions will provide the basis for identifying the ultimate causes of your errors.

If you do not understand all of your errors (or the reasons for your grade) take your exam to the grader or course instructor and go over it with him in detail.

Identify the Causes of Your Errors   Errors will usually fall into one or more of the following categories.

Failures in original study.   If there was material on the test that you never saw before or that you recognized only vaguely, the chances are that you never studied the material, or never studied it thoroughly in the first place. You may not have read all the material, or not understood what you read, or misjudged the importance of what you read. You may not have attended lectures regularly, or may have taken poor notes. (One student, for example, complained that he "could not understand why he did so poorly on the test," even though his test paper showed clearly that he had missed nearly 50 percent of questions dealing with lecture material and only 25 percent of those based on the reading.)

If the evidence indicates that your original studying was inadequate, you are urged to read (or reread) Chapters 2–5 and 11.

Failures in test preparation.   If you wrote an essay with plenty of facts but no organization, or if you had trouble recalling things on the test that you know you originally understood, or if you tried unsuccessfully to outguess the teacher, the chances are that you made errors in test preparation. You may have failed to make exam study notes in order to organize the material in your mind. Perhaps you studied the material enough to understand it, but did not spend enough time programming it into memory. (Did you try to do too much cramming?) Maybe when you thought up hypothetical questions, you assumed that the teacher would ask only the ones you hoped he would ask and no others.

If your problem was one of faulty test preparation, read (or reread) Chapters 6, 7, and 12.

Failures in test-taking technique.   Did you fail to follow the directions for the test? Did you misallocate your time among the various test questions? Did you rush into the essay without thinking and write on the wrong topic or with the wrong theme in mind? Did you make careless errors in cases where you really did know the material? Did you fail to edit your answers? If so, the chances are that your problem lies in the area of test-taking technique. Test anxiety may also have contributed to your poor performance. Read (or reread) the relevant parts of Chapters 12 and 17 for a discussion of these issues.

Miscellaneous factors.   A poor or inappropriate physical or social environment may have contributed to many of the foregoing problems. For example, did you study with too many distractions? Did you try to substitute group study for individual study? Did you schedule too little time for the course in which you failed? Did you waste much of the available time that you did have? If your problems involved any of the above, read (or reread) Chapters 8–10 for suggestions.

Inadequate study monitoring. After you have read or reread some or all of the above chapters, read Chapter 13 on "Study Monitoring," which explains how to insure that you are using proper methods of study.

A list of the key factors responsible for most test failures is given in Table 3. You are advised to go through this list after each test failure and answer each of these 25 questions "yes" or "no." The questions

Table 3. Failure Diagnosis Checklist

1. Were you doing perceptual-level reading when doing the assigned homework? (Chapter 2)
2. Did you fail to understand the basic concepts? (Chapter 3)
3. Did you fail to integrate the concepts and theories with each other? (Chapter 4)
4. Did you fail to pick out and/or designate the important ideas and concepts? (Chapter 5)
5. Did you fail to make "working notes" from the reading? (Chapter 5)
6. Did you attempt "cramming" rather than periodic review of the material? (Chapter 6)
7. Did you fail to program the material into memory (using appropriate methods)? (Chapter 7)
8. Did you study in a location where you were constantly bothered by distractions and interruptions? (Chapter 8)
9. Did you substitute "group study" for mastering the material yourself? (Chapter 9)
10. Did you fail to organize your time properly (waste, overload, etc.)? (Chapter 10)
11. Did you fail to identify clearly the role of lectures in the course? (Chapter 11)
12. Did you fail to take complete lecture notes (errors of omission, etc.)? (Chapter 11)
13. Did you fail initially to study all of the material thoroughly? (Chapter 12)
14. Did you fail to make exam study notes? (Chapter 12)

to which you answer "yes" can be the nucleus around which you formulate your future plan of action (to be discussed shortly).

Causal factors outside your control. Doing poorly on an exam is not always due to factors within your control. There are times when the test questions are unclear and ambiguous; or the questions may be clear but the grading unfair; or the grading itself may be fair but the questions may not cover the material the teacher said would be covered; or the test may be too long for the time allowed.

While these types of problems are frustrating, there is very little you can do about them except to complain to the teacher in charge of the course (see Chapter 16). If this does not help, your best bet is to work on those causal factors that you *can* control rather than "stewing" about those you cannot control.

15. Did you fail to program all the material into memory when preparing for the exam? (Chapter 12)
16. Did you fail to do the practice or homework problems and exercises given out in class or given in your text? (Chapter 12)
17. During the exam did you fail to read the directions or the questions carefully? (Chapter 12)
18. Did you "rush" through the exam without thinking? (Chapters 12 and 17)
19. Did you fail to outline your essays before writing? (Chapter 12)
20. Did you fail to edit your essays and/or to check your answers for accuracy? (Chapter 12)
21. Did you fail to monitor your mental processes adequately when studying (subject, level and type of focus, false conclusions, subjectivism, etc.)? (Chapter 13)
22. Did you feel anxious because you were placing too much or the wrong kind of significance on the exam? (Chapter 17)
23. Did you feel anxious during the exam because you did not know the material to begin with? (Chapter 17)
24. During the exam were you guilty of emotional generalization? Did it make you give up or feel unable to make decisions? (Chapter 17)
25. During the exam did you spend your time worrying rather than focusing on the actual exam questions? (Chapter 17)

Note: In deciding on whether to answer "yes" or "no" to each of these questions, you are advised *not* to give yourself the benefit of the doubt.

Developing a Plan of Action

After you have thoroughly diagnosed your failure and identified its various causes and their relative importance, the next step is to formulate a positive plan of action for achieving success in your next exam (or course or semester). This plan should parallel the diagnostic categories discussed above; that is, it should specify needed modifications in your study methods, your techniques of exam preparation, your test-taking procedures, and relevant miscellaneous factors (time use, etc.). All plans should include a list of things to monitor for (see Chapter 13). As noted above, this plan can be based on the items answered "yes" in Table 3. Did you make a plan of action after your last failure? If not, do it now.

Remotivating Yourself After Failure

After a test failure, you will feel discouraged and unhappy and perhaps reluctant to keep trying. Thus you will be faced with the problem of (re-) arousing and sustaining your study motivation.

Focus on the Benefits of College   One reason you may feel unmotivated is that you have not fully conceptualized in your own mind the benefits to be obtained from a college education. If you *do* view college attendance to be in your self-interest, it is important to remind yourself of the reasons *why* you think it is beneficial to your welfare (see Chapter 14). This requires a conscious identification of your goals (especially long-term goals), of the reasons you chose them, and of their meaning for you.

Hold the Failure in Proper Perspective   It is easy to generalize emotionally from failure (as well as from anxiety, as noted in Chapter 17), and to reach (conscious or subconscious) conclusions such as: "I'll never succeed in this course"; "I'll never be able to do college work"; "I'm stupid and dumb"; "I don't have enough innate ability to do this work"; "I'll probably fail the next test, and then the course, and the flunk out of school which will prove I'm no good"; "There is no point in trying it; it never pays off"; "My parents (friends) will kill me (make fun of me) for this; I'll never live it down."

Learn to limit your conclusions when you fail to what your performance objectively demonstrates. Usually it means that you did not have sufficient knowlege to do well on one or more tests and nothing more. Remember: a few low test grades a semester will not ruin your life; one failure (or even several) does not mean that you lack the ability to do college work (although sometimes a change of courses or of major may be indicated); your parents will not disown you for a poor grade; failing to do as well as you wanted on a test does not prove that effort is futile.

Identify Defensive Reactions   Often a student is prevented from coping rationally with failure by his own refusal to acknowledge that the failure was in any way his own fault. He may blame it on poor working conditions, the unclear textbook, inadequate lectures, the unfairness of the test, biased grading, the intellectual corruption of the university, or even the moral depravity of society as a whole. He may rationalize his failure by trying to convince himself that it is not important anyway since he was never really trying in the first place.

If you recognize that defense mechanisms are ways of evading or distorting reality in order to cater to your whims or feelings, you will see why they prevent you from coping effectively with your problems. How can you cope with failure if you refuse to acknowledge that you failed or that the failure was (at least partly) your fault? If you refuse to identify the real causes of your errors, you will be unable to take corrective action and are doomed to repeat the same mistakes in the future.

While it may hurt at first to acknowledge your own errors, you are much better off in the long run because you are at least in contact with reality instead of living in a fantasy world. (If you become severely depressed after failure, do not hesitate to contact your college health or counseling center immediately.)

Focus on Future Plans   To avoid repeating past failures, as we have noted, you need to identify their causes and develop a plan of action which will eliminate them in the future. Such plans of action not only provide you with knowledge, they help remotivate you as well. By focusing your attention on why past errors occurred and how they can be avoided, such plans build confidence in your ability to cope with future difficulties. It is a great morale booster to know that *past mistakes do not have to be repeated and to know specifically what actions you can take to avoid them.*

Sometimes students become discouraged about planning because they worked very hard for a test and still did poorly on it. Poor test performance, however, is not always due to inadequate time spent in study. It may also result from inappropriate *methods* of study (or exam preparation or test-taking technique). Effort itself will not guarantee success; the effort must be directed properly—that is, *to-*

*ward insuring that your mind is performing the appropriate opera-
tions on the material to be learned.* It is not blind effort but intelligent, purposeful effort that leads to successful academic performance.
(See Part I of this book for details.)

Reevaluate Your Aspirations and Standards of Success   Often students
see themselves as failures, not because they actually did so badly on
a test, but because the standards they use to judge their success are
irrational and unrealistic. It *is* rational to base your standards on what
your college, your scholarship contract, your major department,
and/or your intended graduate school require, since these are demands which must be met in order to attain your future goals. It *is*
rational to set your standards in line with your own past performance,
since this takes into account relevant facts such as your demonstrated
ability, type of major, course load, available study time, personal
problems, and the like.

It is *not* rational to choose another person's performance
(roommate's, brother's, sister's, friend's, etc.) as your standard of success. This procedure involves relinquishing your own judgment and
putting success and failure basically *out of your control.* You cannot
control the abilities, courses, efforts, study techniques, or aspirations
of other persons. Thus if you use their performance as your standard
of comparison, you are, in effect, totally at their mercy when judging
yourself. You will continually feel anxious, because you will never
know where you stand from one day to the next. You will feel constant self-doubt because you will never be sure if you can match the
other person's performance or not.

To feel in control you must think of learning as fundamentally an
issue between *you and reality* (you and the material and the objective requirements of your college, etc.). You should ask yourself: Am
I learning the material? Am I doing the best I can under the circumstances? Are my aspirations realistic? Is my performance good enough
to attain my long-term goals?

If you are dissatisfied with your performance, set a goal to *improve
over your previous performance* and keep raising your goals as you
improve until you are satisfied. This will insure that you have some
control over your success and failure and that no matter where you
start you will have some realistic, attainable goal to aim for. If you are
an entering freshman, you might use your grade average in high
school as a starting point; however, as noted in Chapter 1, college is a
good deal harder than high school, so that you will have to do substantially more work and study more effectively just to maintain your
high school average in college.

Summary

Failure, as defined here, means doing less well in a test or a course than you wanted to do. Failure entails feelings of discouragement, disappointment, and other unpleasant emotions. The first step in coping with failure is to diagnose its causes. These will usually fall into one of three categories—inadequate initial study of the material, improper test preparation, and poor test-taking technique—although other factors such as a poor study environment may be involved. Inadequate study monitoring may also contribute to failure. The next step is to develop a plan of action which will correct and eliminate past errors on subsequent tests. A third problem is remotivating yourself after failure. It requires that you: remind yourself of the benefits of a college education; hold the failure in proper perspective (avoiding emotional generalizations); identify and eliminate any defensive reactions; focus on your future plan of action; and reevaluate your standards of success to insure that they are realistic.

19. Motivational Monitoring

Monitoring is "introspection directed to one's *methods* of mental functioning"[1] (see Chapter 13). It entails the identification and regulation of one's own mental processes. Monitoring is volitional; it is a process which is initiated and sustained by choice.

Chapter 13 discussed using monitoring to insure that one was performing mental operations on study material which would produce learning (i.e., understanding plus memory). The emphasis in the present chapter is on identifying and correcting mental processes (and related mental contents) that undermine or impair study motivation. The purpose of motivational monitoring is to insure that you are avoiding or correcting the types of errors in mental functioning described in the previous five chapters.

What To Monitor For

Awareness of Your Self-Interest   Since your ability to arouse and sustain study motivation depends on your reasons for coming to college,

176   1. A. Blumenthal, "The Base of Objectivist Psychotherapy" (see p. 125).

you need to be constantly aware of why you came and what you expect to get out of college. When considering whether to enter (or to remain in) college or not, what to major in, what courses to take, and why you should keep trying in the face of setbacks, your prime consideration should be your own interests, values, and long-term goals and how each decision will help to attain them (see Chapter 14). Remind yourself that attending college is not a duty, i.e., that *you do not have to go to college!* You only have to go *if* you want certain goals and *if* college is the only way to attain them.

It is especially important when things are not going as well as you would like to remind yourself of why you are here and what you expect to get out of it. This will help to reconfirm and "make real" to you your values and their personal significance.

Passivity Regarding Academic Interests   Are you waiting passively for your preexisting interests to push you into studying, that is, waiting for your feelings to lead, hoping that your mind will follow? If so, it is unlikely that you will ever develop any interests that you did not have before you came to college. On the other hand, if you attempt to understand and familiarize yourself thoroughly with new material which you encounter in your courses, you may find that interests will be aroused and developed through the process of learning (see Chapter 15). This is especially likely to happen when preparing a term paper since you are (presumably) getting into the material in depth and making numerous integrations between your prior knowledge and the new material.

Unresolved Conflicts   As noted in Chapter 15, psychological conflicts can be difficult to identify because they are partially or wholly subconscious. However, to the degree that they are partially conscious or become so through introspection, you may be in a position to take steps to resolve them. Knowing that you have one or more conflicts and failing to take appropriate action may add to the problems caused by the conflicts themselves. For example, if you discover that you did not really want to come to college at all but went only out of duty, failing to act on this knowledge (e.g., deciding whether there are any selfish reasons for you to go, etc.) may increase your feelings of fatigue and make you feel guilty and depressed for not making a firm decision when you know that one needs to be made.

(This does not mean that you should rush into action as soon as you see the glimmer of a psychological conflict. It is best to wait until you understand the conflict clearly before reaching a definite conclusion. Sometimes you may need psychological counseling in order to resolve the issue fully.)

Using Irrational Standards "No matter how well I do on a test, I always feel I should have done better." Thus spoke one student who suffered from intense test anxiety. She was judging herself according to a standard of omniscience, so that nothing short of knowing everything perfectly would do. Since such a standard is impossible to live up to, the student felt anxious and out of control before her tests, and guilty and dissatisfied afterwards. If you catch yourself using such standards to judge yourself, you must remind yourself of *why* they are irrational and reassert a rational standard in their place.

It is also possible to set irrationally low standards (that are way below your ability) so that there will be no chance of failing to reach them (see Chapter 16). Such standards are based on fear of failure rather than hope of success. As such they yield a sense of relief (mixed with guilt) but no real satisfaction when attained.

Standards of achievement based on the accomplishments of others (e.g., parents, siblings, friends, acquaintances) also generate anxiety (as noted in Chapter 17) since they involve relinquishing your own judgment and placing your self-evaluations at the mercy of others. If you find yourself constantly comparing yourself to others and asking others to judge you, remind yourself that how they perform is not a significant issue. What is important is what you do with the ability you have in the context of your personal circumstances (e.g., major, study load, time schedule, health, etc.).

Emotional Generalization Emotional generalization is a process of reaching conclusions (about oneself or some external event or category of events) based on the emotions they elicit and on ideas automatically aroused by or associated with these emotions through habit. For example, a student who cannot answer the first one or two questions on a test, and concludes that he knows nothing and will not be able to answer any of the remaining questions, is letting fear and anxiety determine his conclusions rather than logical deduction from the facts. To combat such a conclusion, the student would have to remind himself that two items do not make a test (in most cases) and that only after he has seen and thought about *all* the items will he be able to determine just how much he knows or does not know.

Similarly, when a student fails to understand some point when he first reads it, he might "feel" stupid and incompetent and conclude that he actually is. To avoid erroneous conclusions in such a case, he would have to consider a variety of alternative hypotheses. For example, he might not have been in full focus when he read the passage; or perhaps the writer of the passage was himself unclear; or perhaps the passage is simply a difficult one so that almost anyone would have to read it several times to understand it fully; or possibly he needs more background study before tackling that particular book.

One student gave a very graphic analogy to illustrate how emotional generalization influenced his attitude toward exams: "I look at [tests] as if they were a row of dominoes—mess up one and everything falls down." This was the conclusion which his emotions reached. To reach rational conclusions about the significance of exams, you have to use your mind.

A student who fails a test may feel that doomsday is just around the corner, but if he rationally analyzed the real meaning of his failure, he would reach quite different conclusions, e.g., he failed to study the material thoroughly; he used the wrong methods of exam preparation; he made errors in test-taking technique (see Chapter 18). Rather than signifying the end of the world, the low grade may simply mean that he will have to work harder or more effectively for the next test (or in other courses, or during the next semester, etc.).

Another form of emotional generalization is regulating your work in a course solely according to how much you personally like or dislike the teacher. The "thought" process in the latter case goes: "If he's going to be a jerk like that, I'll be damned if I'll do any work for him." The error lies in transferring the feelings you have about the teacher to the material he teaches. Even if you wanted to "get even" for some alleged injustice, refusing to work in the course is not the way to do it, since your low grade will certainly not hurt the teacher's feelings. It will only hurt you. Furthermore, there may be something worthwhile you can learn even from the worst of teachers.

If you like the teacher, there is no problem, since working hard in a course will only help your performance. (However, if you spend so much time on this one course that it detracts from your performance in other courses, you can still end up in academic trouble.)

Giving up is frequently a consequence of emotional generalization, e.g., "Trying hard did not work on the last test, so why should it work in the future?" "I tried hard without success on this course, so why try in any course?" "Since I can't understand this passage after reading it three times, I'll never understand it." "I can't do the first question on this test, so I probably can't do any of them." In these cases the students have focused on their feelings of the moment and generalized them to all superficially similar circumstances.

Emotional generalization typically involves a *distortion of time perspective* (i.e., a dropping of temporal context). The future is so dominated or blocked out by the present that nothing is real except the emotions of the moment and their associated conclusions. It is as if one held the conscious premise: "If I can't get what I want *now*, to hell with everything (or: everything is hell)." Holding context in the face of aversive emotions requires a conceptual identification of the erroneous conclusions one is making (or starting to make) and a conscious self-reminder to the effect that there *is* a tomorrow and that one will take it into account when making decisions. The ability to do this consistently is the hallmark of psychological maturity. More specifically, doing it consistently is the means by which you become mature.

Defense Mechanisms A defense mechanism is a device whereby one distorts one's perception of reality (including oneself) in order to reduce or avoid guilt, anxiety, or other unpleasant emotions. One common defense mechanism involves avoiding self-blame for errors, character flaws, or irrational actions by attributing them to others. For example, a student who did poorly on an exam as the result of inadequate study and was unwilling to admit this fact to himself might blame his problem on the unfair test, biased grading, poor study conditions, lack of sleep, or distractions in the classroom (see Chapter 18).

Another common defense mechanism involves trying to explain away irrational actions by making up "plausible" excuses or rationalizations. For example, a student may encounter difficult material and make no attempt to deal with it at all. He will simply skip over it, saying to himself, "To save time, I'll come back to that later—maybe the night before the exam." This is usually a rationalization, because the student never intends to go back to it, and he knows it. The real reason he skipped it was that he did not want to bother with it. What he is secretly hoping is that if he denies the existence of the difficult passage, it will somehow go away or enter his brain without study. Of course, it won't and doesn't, so he pays the price on the exam.

Often studying will be postponed repeatedly while time is frittered away on nonessential activities which one pretends are important. Or one may study in poor surroundings on the grounds that "there's no other choice" when, in fact, one simply does not want to change one's routine. Or one may skip or pay no attention to lectures on the grounds that "they are not important," when in truth one really wanted to play cards or frisbee instead.

To understand the power of defense mechanisms to control your choices and actions, you must first observe them in action and then identify them for what they are, namely forms of self-deception.

Resorting to such mechanisms is obviously not in your rational self-interest. By distorting the facts, or not facing up to them fully, you deny yourself the possibility of identifying the real causes of your problems. If you fail to identify the real causes, you will not be able to correct the problems. You will be allowing yourself to live in a fantasy world, where problems lead to defenses which lead to more problems, promoting further defenses and so on.

Summary

Motivational monitoring involves detecting and correcting errors in thinking that block or undermine one's motivation to study. Examples of such errors include: failing to focus on the selfish benefits of attending college; waiting passively to be pushed into study by one's preexisting interests; ignoring unresolved conflicts; using irrational standards to judge oneself and one's scholastic performance; using emotional generalization to reach conclusions; and using defense mechanisms which distort reality.

20. Autobiographical Portraits of Two Self-motivated Students

This chapter consists of brief autobiographical sketches of two college students, one male and one female. The sketches are focused on the students' educational histories. I asked these particular students to write about themselves because both had to overcome difficult obstacles in order to achieve their educational goals. I call them "self-motivated" students because they *did* overcome these obstacles through their own efforts. In this respect these sketches illustrate the operation of human volition.

Each sketch is followed by brief comments which serve to integrate the autobiographical material with the material in Chapters 14–19. All proper names (and some minor facts) have been changed in order to protect the identity of the students involved.

The reader may find it illuminating to read through these sketches and to compare these students' attitudes, motives, and techniques of coping with stress and frustration with his or her own.

Shelley Carlson

In high school my interest in school reached an all-time low.
182 Because of the attitudes of young people ages 14–18, the classroom

atmosphere tended to be disruptive and consequently not serious
(e.g., more time is spent disciplining rowdy pupils than teaching).
Most important, the quality of teachers and hence the quality of
teaching was so pathetically poor at Mt. Morgan High School that it's
frightening to think that Pocono County schools are supposed to be
among the nation's best.

The result of all this in terms of my attitude was that I simply
didn't care about learning anything in high school. I just wanted to
get it over with, but the actual process was boring me. Because I did
want to go to college though, I did maintain a B average but, beyond
this, I had almost no motivation to achieve in high school.

Eventually, I was singled out by my teachers and guidance
counselor as a problem student. As a result, the expectation of
everyone was that I should be a C or D student, and that I was
definitely not college material. Even when I would disconfirm these
grade expectations, their attitude, that I was not college material,
persisted.

My high school guidance counselor, Mr. Legget, called me into his
office periodically for a lecture on my "bad" attitude. I had the
capacity, he would tell me, to be an A student, to be another Peggy
Smith. (Peggy was a very bright, involved student—probably one of
the best in the school.) I would usually reply that I was and always
would be Shelley Carlson, that the idea of being "another" anyone
else didn't inspire me. Mr. Legget finally "advised" me not to waste
my time going to college, because I would flunk out.

When I proposed applying to Midland U., he told me that I would
be wasting my application fee, because I wouldn't be accepted. I
applied anyway. One of my most gratifying moments in high school
was going to his office and dropping my letter of acceptance on his
desk!

By June when I graduated from high school, I was really looking
forward very much to college. Unfortunately in July I had a bad car
accident. Because I had suffered a brain injury that would take a year
to heal completely, my neurosurgeon advised me not to go to school
for a year as the brain injury had mental and emotional
repercussions (e.g., limited concentration span, forgetfulness,
nervousness, and just a general state of mental confusion). The
symptoms of the brain injury, though, were subtle in the sense that
at the time I wouldn't seem to an outsider as though there were
anything wrong with me, and I felt that there was nothing really
wrong with me.

The way I found out the real extent of my injuries was by starting
Midland U. that September (against my doctor's orders). Once in

school, I was struggling just to get Cs and Ds. In November, I decided to withdraw from school before I did permanent damage to my college record and to return in September of the following year. After withdrawing from school, I stayed home for a month and commiserated with myself about having had to withdraw from school. By January I'd had enough commiserating. My initial relief at being free from the pressure of school turned into boredom with doing nothing. So I got a job as a bookkeeper in a bank.

The job, as much as I hated it, was a valuable experience. The work I was doing was mindless—it wasn't something I got any satisfaction out of. It was just something I did for eight hours a day, because it was employment. This experience showed me that what I wanted from an occupation was to get some satisfaction out of doing the work and that, for me, meant using my mind. In spite of my dislike for the job, I kept it until May, because at the time I had no viable alternatives—I could either go back home and do nothing, or quit the job and look for another that would probably be essentially the same type of work.

In May, I left that job, and decided to take the summer off. This gave me lots of time to think. In the light of all the experiences over the past year or so, I had a lot to think about. It seems to me that more than anything else, the conclusions I came to at that point were most significant in determining my present attitudes. That is, I think I could have had all the same experiences and yet, without these few months with a lot of time alone to think and synthesize my ideas, there's a good possibility that I would have been completely different now. Here are the conclusions I came to in chronological order of the events that led to them.

The only thing I feel I learned in high school is that other people's evaluations of me were not necessarily correct. So even though high school was academically a waste of four years, it was invaluable just because it taught me that simple little fact.

After spending two months recovering from the car accident in a sort of idleness (no obligations, responsibilities, etc.), I learned that the condition of "carefree" idleness is far from being ideal; rather it's the antithesis of living. After a while I felt as though I were living in a vacuum. This little lesson is really a help when I'm under all the tension and pressure of school and exams. In the midst of it all I can stop and remember that no matter how great the tension is and no matter how much I want to escape it, that all this is part of life, that the alternative—doing nothing—or the next best alternative—halfway doing something—are not what life is about for me.

Working in the bank, I experienced the occupational alternative to college, and spending the summer in the apartment in the role of "lady of the house" [Shelley's mother was away], I experienced the nonoccupational alternative to college and/or having a profession.

In a sense, then, I had a brief taste of a couple of different lifestyles and arrived, partly by a process of elimination, at my choice of going into a profession. But more than this I want to have a profession because I value and enjoy using my mind, using it doing things I consider more significant than punching an adding machine or waxing the floor. Because my chosen profession interests me, and because there are still a lot of unanswered questions in that field, I want it to be my profession.

Although I was looking forward to starting school in the fall, I was also somewhat anxious about going to school again, having had to operate at somewhat less than full mental capacity for a year because of the brain injury; and, more specifically, not having been able to succeed in college previously had left me somewhat unnerved as far as meeting intellectual challenges was concerned.

In dealing with my anxiety, I resorted to a technique I had developed over the past year for handling difficulties. I use the word technique, or maybe more accurately method, because the way I solved and still solve problems was something consciously thought about and implemented. The first thing I did was to recognize the problem in its simplest and most elementary aspects and consciously confront it.

My problem, in essence, was that despite my genuine interest in learning, I was anxious over whether or not I would be able to live up to my own standards in school. I wanted to be able to just find out about a lot of things I knew very little about—government, math, sociology, science, etc. I didn't want to know things for any particular purpose. I just wanted to know about these things for myself.

My anxiety at this time, I guess, was twofold. First, I was anxious about whether or not I would be true to myself and really work honestly for my goal, i.e., to learn everything I could as well as I could. Then I was worried about whether or not I would be able to earn the grades I needed to stay in school.

Once I had confronted my problem I realized, first, that the only person who had any control over whether or not I met my own goal was me. Second, I decided that I had the ability to achieve my goals. Then, third, and probably most important, I made a commitment to myself that I would do what was necessary to achieve my goals. Quite simply then, the method I used to deal with my anxiety about school was, first, realizing that I was the only one who could solve the problem; second, that I had the ability to solve the problem; and, third, that I *would* solve the problem.

After I resolved the broader aspects of the situation, I got down to the practical realities of how to go about achieving my goals. I read a book about how to study in college and came up with a "plan of attack" for approaching different subjects. I worked out a rough time schedule for myself so that I could make realistic plans, etc. I bought a large table and set up a "study area" in my room and just generally got myself ready for school.

The reason I stress my method or formula for problem-solving so much is that it has been somewhat of a guiding light to me in my educational process. For me, it was a breakthrough, in that figuring it out was a conscious effort and discovering it was in a real sense an "aha" experience. I was really amazed at how uncomplicated and elementary my method was—confront the problem and make a commitment to solve it. The conception that I was the only person who could solve this, and later many other personal problems, I found to be very comforting and even rather exhilarating.

I feel as though it may still seem somewhat unclear why I consider my little formula so important, so I'll try to clarify it through a brief practical example. I know people who have the same ability I do who, when grades come out, exclaim to me," Wow—how do you do it?" in a tone that seems to imply that there must be something mystical about it. When I answer that you just make up your mind you want to do it and then just do it, they either seem befuddled or answer something like, "It's not that easy for me." The misunderstanding may be that my solution is *simple* but not *easy*.

When I come across one of those seemingly impossible courses that inevitably happens once a semester, or when I'm in the middle of exam week with my semester goal being a 4.0, I sit down and engage in a few minutes of consciously evaluating the problem—almost like giving myself a talk. I think about the fact that I'm in school by choice, that I want to learn, that I'm the only one who can achieve that goal for myself, that I can achieve it, and that I will achieve it. Somehow after these little "bull sessions" with myself, no matter how seemingly impossible the task (Constitutional Law, Statistics, etc.), I feel really "on top of it," and I am able to do things that really still astound me—studying Law 10 hours a day for 5 days, studying Personality Theory in 14-hour stretches, etc.

Possibly most important, to me at least, is that even when I'm really struggling with something at school, once I make up my mind to really, honestly learn everything I can, even though the rest is hard work, I am really satisfied with the feeling of gratification I have while doing it. Gratification doesn't adequately describe the feeling though. It's just a certain sense of "being" I get when I've made, or in a sense, renewed my commitment and I'm working to achieve what I want.

Let me sum up, then, the basic attitudes that have to this point motivated me in college. First, and probably most important, is that I am here by choice; right now there is nothing else I want to do but be in college *learning*. And I have made a commitment to myself to gain maximally in a personal way from everything I do. For me, with reference to college, that means to commit myself firmly to my goal of learning and to work to attain those goals. So the big question may be, "So why do you do all that work and get so involved in school?" The answer is that I do it because I enjoy it—not in the blissful, carefree, easy way that the word "enjoy" usually implies. Rather, I enjoy it in the sense that I enjoy that indescribable sense of being, of living, that I experience when I've made a personal commitment to something I value and am honestly working to maintain that commitment.

Shelley's grade averages for her four years of college were, respectively, B, B+, A, and A. She now plans to attend graduate school in furtherance of her career objectives.

Comments   One of Shelley's most prominent characteristics is her active pursuit of her goals in the face of external obstacles. She is, in effect, the opposite of a "psychological determinist" (see Chapter 16). She seeks to control events instead of letting events control her. In high school she maintained a B average despite the excruciating boredom of her courses. She applied to college despite the negative recommendation of her guidance counselor. She started college in spite of a recent brain injury (a decision which proved mistaken at the time, but which turned out all right in the long run). She developed her own technique of arousing herself to greater effort when frustrated by difficult courses in college.

Shelley's self-assertiveness was not confined to the realm of action but was also present in the realm of thought. (Actually, the latter was the cause of the former.) She took time to draw conclusions actively from her experiences. She observed in high school that other people's evaluations of her were not always correct. She learned from her work experience and from her experience as "woman of the house" that these roles were not for her. She learned from being idle that only a career which involved the full use of her mind would be satisfying to her. She learned how to cope with anxiety by actively applying a technique of problem-solving she had discovered earlier (e.g., breaking the problem down into its basic elements, etc.). When she needed more information about a subject, she went out and got it (e.g., she bought a book on how to study to prepare herself for college).

Observe that Shelley's method of reaching conclusions about herself and the world was the antithesis of emotional generalization (see Chapters 18 and 19). She did not allow her feelings to run wild while her mind followed passively. She attempted to identify the meaning of her experiences conceptually and emotional control followed. Despite her anxieties she made a firm commitment to her goals because this was necessary in order to attain them.

The active use of her conscious judgment enabled Shelley to develop a firm sense of herself. In high school she refused to subvert her own identity by trying to become "another Peggy Smith." The standards she used to judge her own academic performance were based on her judgment of the objective requirements of the situation (she aimed for Bs in high school in order to be able to get into college); and on her own past performance (when she attended college for the second time she was initially concerned with doing well enough to stay in and, presumably, do better than she had before). She did not blindly accept others' judgments of her if they contradicted her own judgment. She entered college by her own choice and in order to pursue her own goals. At first the goal was to satisfy her intellectual curiosity. Later she developed specific career aspirations and went on to pursue them. She recognized that she was the only one who could control whether or not she attained her own goals and that she had the ability to reach them.

For these reasons Shelley Carlson is properly described as a self-motivated student.

How would you compare Shelley Carlson to yourself? How are you similar to her in terms of your approach to college study? How are you different? What can you learn from her?

Jim Johnson

In the third grade I never received any grade below an A. The other kids told me it wouldn't last—and it didn't. Throughout grades four, five, and six, I never applied myself. I admired kids who did well scholastically, and there were certain ways in which I wanted to emulate them; but most of them were girls, and I had the idea that masculine pursuits were more along the line of physical things (like sports). As a result I actually felt more masculine if I deliberately did poorly in school.

In the sixth grade I experienced a crisis, because I got my first C, and it was in science. This particular time in history coincided with the launching of the first Russian "Sputnik." Pressure came on me from parents, teachers, and even fellow students to start getting good marks. Not surprisingly, math and science quickly became my weakest subjects. I think it was a rebellion against the pressure I was feeling.

I had always had a natural bent for the humanities: literature, art, music, etc. At this time there was a real budding interest in the world of art about to surface, but I tried to kill it. According to the (wrong) premises I had acquired, art too was a feminine interest.

When I entered seventh grade, I felt that everything would be different, because I was attending a new school. I thought a new environment could somehow change my old study habits. I tried to emulate people who really seemed to be on top of their work. I thought that all I had to do was to copy their methods, and I too could succeed scholastically. My focus, however, was on nonessentials. I never made an effort to identify conceptually the reasons for other students' success. I was frozen on a perceptual level, e.g., on their visible actions and eccentricities. One boy would take elaborate pains making artistic covers for his workbooks, so I did the same; but I never quite earned the marks that he did. Another brilliant boy used to do math assignments in ink, making messy chicken scratches whenever he made a mistake. I found that copying this technique did little or nothing to improve my proficiency with numbers.

Since I had gotten nowhere by imitating other kids, I decided that in a contest between passively following their lead and passively doing nothing, doing nothing was better. I "turned off" to bright people, telling myself that it was because they were "cold," "dispassionate," or "insecure"; but the truth was that it was simply easier not to think.

When I first entered high school, my anxiety at being an academic underachiever was eased somewhat by an increased concentration on playing the trumpet. I did, in fact, enjoy it, but I think it was to some extent a way of "blotting out" my feeling of failure in school. I went out of my way to participate in all types of musical performances, bands, dances, etc., so I could have the sense of feeling good at something.

I joined the high school band so I could spend more time playing music. As I broadened my musical interests, my grades plummeted.

I received a D in math; but I never let myself go down the drain completely. Eventually I was on the honor roll again, but through it all I had horrible study habits and did everything I could to avoid study. School for me was the dullest thing in the world. I didn't know what I wanted to do, but I could not imagine that it would be anything that I would need my school lessons for.

By this time I had acquired a strong habit of passivity. You could break down my passivity as follows: 1. I perceive a situation as threatening in some way. 2. I "defend" myself against this threat by blotting the unpleasantness out of my mind, e.g., by daydreaming in class so that I would not hear what the teacher said. 3. A type of pretentiousness would set in that would enable me to feel superior in some way to the teacher, e.g., I was young, innocent, minding my own business, and he was a hostile aggressor always trying to dominate me and control my thoughts. I grew to resent all teachers. 4. In the evenings when I didn't have sufficient knowledge to prepare an assignment, I felt a mixture of guilt and fear which I dealt with in the following ways: (a) watching TV or some other activity that would take my mind off it; (b) deceiving myself into believing that it didn't matter how I did in school; and (c) vowing to myself that at some point in the future I would change my ways—"I'll do better next time." 5. The next day when I didn't have my work done, I would feel horribly inferior. In a few cases I even tried to cheat, but I was never able to improve my grades this way. I only succeeded in lowering my self-esteem further and making myself feel like a thoroughly fraudulent and worthless person.

By the time I graduated from high school I had decided to pursue a musical career. I chose to study at a liberal arts college rather than a musical conservatory. Undoubtedly one of the reasons behind attending a liberal arts college was the fear that I would become too narrow in my interests at a conservatory. I felt "safer" someplace where there was a lot of academic work in liberal arts courses, because I thought the professor might "pull me along" and make me able to think critically about such subjects by osmosis. Of course, this didn't happen. I got frustrated and disgusted with my C grades in college.

I blamed my failures on bad professors, poor choice of curriculum, a bad advisor, a crummy environment, etc. The truth was that I refused to be self-motivated. When I took a course in Introductory Psychology, I kept waiting for the professor to get "interesting." I rationalized my failures by telling myself, in effect, "Psychology is not an important subject for a musician. After all, music takes up a lot of time." But the fact was that I was not spending my free time on music. I was running around with friends, etc.

I began to retreat further and further away from academic life. My average slid to below a C, so that my grades would not have permitted me to transfer to another institution (e.g., a conservatory) even if I had wanted to.

Anxiety began to increase as the cold hard fact began to hit me that I could go nowhere without good grades. If I ever wanted to teach music in college, for example, I would need a Master's degree. I became more and more resentful of my professors. It was always *them—they* kept me from doing well. Of course, this was again a rationalization. I couldn't bring myself to admit that it was my own passivity that was getting me into trouble.

In addition, I was locked into my long, unhappy pattern of failures, because when a person builds up years of habit, it has a cumulative effect on him. I tried many times to apply myself to my books in the evening, but it seemed almost impossible to do well. I remember at the end of my junior year, I stayed up all night in a do-or-die effort to study for a music history test. I tried outlining with notes and forcing myself to concentrate and memorize important dates and terms. So extreme was this contrast from my normal pattern that I woke up feeling deathly ill after an hour or so of sleep and vomited. I could not take the exam the next day and had to make it up later.

I finally did improve my study efforts and made better than a B average in the first semester of my senior year. But in trying to choose a graduate school I was nearly panic-stricken. I tried to cram several courses into the spring semester that I thought would impress graduate schools, but I did poorly in them. I think it was a problem of trying to do well in a course so that it would impress someone else that interfered with my progress. I did graduate that spring but with a [cumulative] average of slightly above C. Not surprisingly, it wasn't acceptable to any graduate school, and that summer I had absolutely no place to go.

I had become bitter and resentful toward the whole world the summer after I got my degree. For most of the summer I sat around and did nothing. I was trying to blame everything on some other influence or cause. I kept thinking to myself, "Why didn't anyone ever tell me that this would happen?"

The fall came and I was told that if I enrolled as a "special student" in my alma mater, I would be considered for admission to their graduate school, provided I did well as a special student. I immediately accepted, but I had to take a course from the most notoriously vague and unclear professor in the school. Even though I made some (but not much) effort, I was eventually dismissed on his recommendation as "definitely not graduate school material."

I was desolated. It seemed like the end. I went to see my graduate advisor, and he told me that there was little hope of getting back in. He told me that, if I wished, I could write a special letter to the graduate committee asking for consideration, but there was no guarantee that they would agree to it. I decided to write the letter and pick up the pieces of what seemed like a shattered life. I went to study with one of the best trumpet teachers in the country, and he told me that my passivity in school work had carried over to my trumpet study, and that I must practice at least five hours a day if I wanted to remain with him. I put forth immense effort and made excellent progress by the end of the summer.

In the fall I went back to college, and the graduate school agreed to give me one more chance. But I had to take a course with the most dreaded professor in the school. And to top it off, he was teaching his stiffest course—you were expected to know every single fact that was contained in the textbook, which ran to more than 800 pages. I had bitten off a mouthful. At this point I felt that there was no way one could surmount such an obstacle unless he were already in possession of good study habits, which I was not.

However, a number of factors made me determined to succeed this time. For one, it was clearly my last chance in the academic world. Second, I had had a taste of the consequences of not having a degree through a number of odd jobs I had held. I concluded that I would not be able to do anything I really wanted without a graduate degree. Thirdly, I had been severely shaken by a couple of anxiety attacks, one of which required temporary hospitalization (for severe stomach cramps caused by "nerves"). Finally, I was thoroughly fed up with the kind of person I had been and was convinced that I had to change and that I would change. (A psychiatrist whom I had been seeing helped me to identify some of these issues.)

When I returned to graduate school, the two things I kept in mind were: *you must not be passive,* and *you must handle the situation rationally.* (My previous brief encounter with graduate school had shown me that I was dominated by my emotions in important ways. For example, when the professor handed back a paper with a low mark on it, I seethed inside—I hated him, blamed him, resented him for doing it, and I never even bothered to analyze the nature of my mistakes, or why I had gotten the low mark. I knew that there was every chance of this happening again in the course I was about to take, so I told myself that I must use this as a learning experience. I must recognize my arrogant feeling of superiority for what it was: as simply a means of getting a false sense of self-esteem, and stop feeling fear about learning what the professor had to say.)

I bought the textbook, and I went to the first class. I knew that I had developed the habit of not listening and was determined to break it. I hung on every word and wrote down every term. The professor scrawled the names of some books and pamphlets on the board that he said "we might look at." I went out and bought them the next day. Every day and every night, if only for a little while, I forced myself to read that text.

I discovered that there were different ways of reading something. You could read something with simply the intention of retaining or memorizing it, or you could read it with the intention of making it a part of you—asking yourself all the questions about the subject that the author had not asked himself, remembering, after all, that he was writing about things that really happened and that they had to have causes. I decided that this attitude must be what it means to be "intellectual," and I liked it.

My classroom habits and attitudes began to change radically. It seemed odd to feature going to school as the main thing in my life—it seemed somehow useless to sit at a drug store soda fountain and snatch a few moments to read my music history text. But it felt so damn good to be on top of something for once that I kept going. I had been mute for years in the classroom, but now I nearly dominated the discussions, asking questions, making comments, asking for subtle clarifications. No one was ever more worried about an exam than I was about the first exam I took, and nobody was ever happier than I was when it came back with an A on it.

Everyone had to do a class lecture on an opera. I didn't know it at the time I chose it, but the opera I selected had never been recorded in its entirety. The other students relied on LP recordings for the bulk of their presentations, but I could not. Our library had only a piano version of it printed in 1896, and some vocal selections from it recorded in the 1920s. So I went to other libraries for information, and presented the plot orally, and played the overture on the piano. At the end I received many compliments for my presentation. In addition, I got an A on my term paper, which I spent many long hours writing, and an A in the course.

Of course after I had been successful (for the first time within

memory) with a difficult course and a difficult professor, it greatly
boosted my confidence, and I felt ready to try it again. It was the
elimination of my passivity and pretensions that had enabled me to
do well, and I was determined to keep them eliminated.

I remember writing the word "active" on a piece of paper and
hanging it on my wall, because I wanted a constant reminder as to
the key to my success. It was amazing how rapidly one thing led to
another, because being active in the sphere of studying enabled me
to think and behave more actively in other areas of my life as well. I
became active in student government associations; I began to seek
out professors in my spare moments to talk with them; and I read
books that were related to my field, but not even required. I
perpetually felt "on top of things," and school became an activity
that I began to enjoy more than anything else I did.

For the first time I began to realize what a tragic joke it had been
on myself to try to blindly "follow the lead" of others, regardless of
who they are, because they can be very wrong, and one never knows
it unless one develops the power of careful, critical thinking and
evaluation, a trait which demands a profoundly active state of mind.

The next semester I got an A average.

Jim attained an overall A− average in graduate school and obtained his Master's degree. He is now a music instructor at a mid-
western university.

Comments   Jim Johnson's story differs from Shelley Carlson's in one
important respect: Jim was, at first, considerably more passive in
dealing with his problems than was Shelley, and as a result it took
him much longer to resolve them than it took her. Jim did not
achieve control over his study habits and study motivation until he
reached graduate school (which he was very fortunate to reach at all).

Up through college, passivity was, in fact, Jim's most characteristic
trait and was manifested in many ways. He waited for the environment to change his study habits; he chose not to think because it was
easier than thinking; he watched TV and daydreamed rather than
study; he waited for his psychology professor to make him interested; he avoided thinking about unpleasant situations, and so on.

This passivity had other consequences. Jim became a thoroughgo-
ing psychological determinist. Having relinquished the responsibility of self-generated thought, he felt that his life was basically out of
his control (which, given his deterministic attitude, it was). If he did
poorly in school it was always caused by the poor courses, a

"crummy" environment, or hostile and unfair teachers. He waited for other people to make him interested or to get him to study "by osmosis." He felt "locked in" to his pattern of poor academic performance.

Jim's determinism was coupled with a defensive attitude that led him to blame others openly for his problems, mistakes, and poor performance in school. It was always them, never him, who were at fault. Jim generalized this attitude even beyond school and became "bitter and resentful toward the whole world."

This defensive attitude naturally produced a low capacity to cope with failure. Having rationalized his failures by claiming that they were caused by others rather than himself, he did not make any effort to discover what he had done to cause them—and hence did not formulate plans of action to correct his past errors.

Jim's passivity also precluded gaining a firm sense of himself and his own identity. From an early age he tried (or wanted) to emulate others. When his values conflicted with those of others, e.g., good scholastic performance and art versus the conventional (and wrong) view of masculinity (sports, poor scholastic performance), he submerged his own values almost without a fight. He tried to copy other students blindly when doing his homework rather than discovering how to study for himself. (This perceptual level focus, e.g., making artistic covers for workbooks in order to get good grades, was another consequence of Jim's passivity.)

Jim only began to think seriously about himself and his problems when his life started to go down the drain, i.e., after his dismissal from graduate school, his anxiety attacks, etc. The second time he entered graduate school he made two commitments to himself: he would not be passive, and he would use reason rather than emotion (e.g., anger, fear) to guide his choices and actions.

He monitored the level and subject of his focus during lectures so that he was aware of everything that was being said. He read his textbook a little each day so that he would not be faced with cramming it all into memory at the last minute. He discovered abstract integrative reading (i.e., conceptual reading) on his own, contrasting it with the perceptual-level and concrete-bound reading he had been doing before (i.e., rote memorization). He took this same attitude into the classroom; he initiated discussions, asked questions, and requested subtle conceptual clarifications of terms.

The result of this policy was not an immediate disappearance of his anxiety; because of the many bad habits and premises he had acquired over the years, Jim still did not feel totally in control. But he maintained his commitment to being active and rational through it all and attained an A in his first course and excellent grades in his subsequent courses.

The eventual results were a heightened sense of self-esteem (because he was now in control of his life); increased confidence (because he proved that he could cope with difficult courses); and a firmer sense of his own identity (because he was now thinking for himself instead of following others passively).

While Jim Johnson started out as a passive, anxious young man who did not know what he wanted or how to attain it, he ended up as an actively self-motivated student.

Do any of Jim Johnson's problems resemble yours? If so, do you "cope" with them the same way he did before he became self-motivated? What can you learn from Jim's discoveries about himself? From his method of resolving his problems?

Index

Notes

Notes

Notes

Notes

Notes

Notes

Notes